Helion & Company Limited
Unit 8 Amherst Business Centre
Budbrooke Road
Warwick
CV34 5WE
England
Tel. 01926 499 619
Email: info@helion.co.uk
Website: www.helion.co.uk
Twitter: @helionbooks
Visit our blog http://blog.helion.co.uk/

Text © Philippe Wodka-Gallien 2023
Photographs © as individually credited
Colour profiles © David Bocquelet,
    Anderson Subtil and Tom Cooper 2023
Maps © Tom Cooper and Anderson Subtil
    2023

Designed and typeset by Farr out
    Publications, Wokingham, Berkshire
Cover design Paul Hewitt, Battlefield Design
    (www.battlefield-design.co.uk)

ISBN 978-1-804512-13-5

British Library Cataloguing-in-Publication
    Data
A catalogue record for this book is available
    from the British Library

We always welcome receiving book
proposals from prospective authors.

CONTENTS

MAP OF EUROPE 1945–1992

Note: In order to simplify the use of this book, all names, locations and geographic designations are as provided in *The Times World Atlas*, or other traditionally accepted major sources of reference, as of the time of described events.

ABBREVIATIONS

ASMP	*Air-sol moyenne portée* (Medium-range air-to-surface missile)
CEA	*Commissariat à l'Energie Atomique* (French Atomic Energy Commission)
CEA-DAM	French Atomic Energy Commission – Military Applications Division
CEA/DAM	*Service de Physique Nucléaire* (Nuclear Physics Service)
CEP	French Centre for Prospectives and Evaluation
CNES	French National Space Agency
CNRS	French National Scientific Research Centre
COFAS	*Commandement des Forces Aériennes Stratégiques* (French Strategic Air Forces)
CSEM	*Centre Saharien d'Expérimentation Militaire* (Saharan Military Experimentation Centre)

DAM	Military Applications Division of the CEA
DGA	Armament Directorate (of the French Ministry of Defence)
DMA	French Ministry of Defence
IAEA	International Atomic Energy Agency
INSTN	*Institut national des sciences et techniques nucléaires* (National Institute for Nuclear Science and Technology)
IPN	*Institut de Physique Nucléaire* (French Institute for Nuclear Physics)
ONERA	French National Aerospace Research Organisation
SSBN	nuclear-powered ballistic missile submarine
SSN	nuclear-powered attack submarine
UNGG	French National Uranium Graphite Gas reactor

INTRODUCTION

Brest, Britany. Facing us, the operational facility of four ballistic missile submarines, or SSBNs. At Saint-Dizier, in eastern France, two Rafale fighter squadrons are trained for a long-range strategic mission. At sea, sailing from Toulon, is an aircraft-carrier – the *Charles de Gaulle* – and its air wings. As regards weapons, M51 ballistic nuclear missiles are in the submarines, and ASMP-A medium yield missiles tucked under the aircraft. This represents the French nuclear force. The *Force océanique stratégique* (Strategic Oceanic Force, or FOST) maintains three vessels in its operational cycle, one of them at sea, somewhere in the deep blue of the ocean. A fourth is undergoing scheduled maintenance in Brest. Each ship is loaded with 16 nuclear missiles, each with a range of about 5,000 miles. Each missile contains several warheads, up to six. The French Air Force's Rafale fleet is attached to the *Forces aériennes stratégiques* (the FAS, or Strategic Air Forces). The FAS is operational on a 24/7 basis. Nuclear-capable Rafale fighters are also in the French Navy. At sea, the *Charles de Gaulle* is the forward base of the *Force aéronavale nucléaire*, or FANU, completing the shadow of the nuclear threat. The autonomy of the Rafale can be extended by a fleet of tankers, the A330 Phénix currently under delivery. After the ignition of its propulsion, the ASMP-A missile can reach its target from a distance of hundreds of miles. FAS Rafales have demonstrated their ability to carry out long-distance non-stop raids lasting more than nine hours and to deliver precision weaponry, as during the allied Operation *Hamilton* in April 2018 in Syria.

In the wake of these vessels and aircraft are no less than some 80 years of relentless labour in the nuclear universe, in the operational nuclear art and in the enduring achievements of aeronautics and astronautics. We invite you to join this trip through military France, from the 1940s to the end of the first Cold War.

The resurrected memory of the French nuclear project
The present book has benefited from the selfless academic research developed by the *Groupe d'études français d'histoire de l'armement nucléaire,* (GREFHAN), an association of historians strongly supported by the French Ministry of Defence. Its role was essential in the reconstruction of the French national nuclear narrative.

Created at the end of the 1980s, GREFHAN represents the French branch of an international academic movement, the Nuclear History Program. Its initiative can be linked to Professor Ernest May of Harvard University in the USA and Uwe Nerlich of the *Stiftung Wissenschaft und Politik* (German Institute for International and Security Affairs). The presidency of GREFHAN has been entrusted to Professor Maurice Vaisse of the *Service historique des armées*, the Directorate for History of the Armed Forces. Its offices are located in the Château de Vincennes, east of Paris. This castle's thick walls, built during the Middle Ages, house the Directorate. Maurice Vaisse's ambition is to turn GREFHAN into the French 'memory tool' on military nuclear issues, focusing on the pioneers of the nuclear era in the 1930s and the structuring decisions taken by France immediately after 1945 under the regime of the *IVe République*.

This French initiative received the support of many qualified personalities, among them Pierre Messmer, Minister of the Armed Forces from 1960–69 under General de Gaulle's tenure, then Prime Minister under the presidency of Georges Pompidou. In addition, the group gathered General François Maurin, who was the first commander of the FAS, Admiral Marcel Duval (chairman of the National Defence Study Committee in the 1980s) and Jean-Baptiste Duroselle of the *Académie des sciences morales et politiques*. Within a few years, GREFHAN produced a comprehensive documentation on the history of the 'French bomb'. In 1985, the French historiography was enriched by a foundational work, *L'aventure atomique, de Gaulle et la dissuasion* (The Atomic Adventure, de Gaulle and Deterrence). This collective work is based on the minutes of a symposium, organised by the University of Franche-Comté and the Charles de Gaulle Institute, which brings together all key actors of the French nuclear project. Since its inception, GREFHAN has made it possible for the general public to discover a rare history whose richness had previously been completely ignored. In September 1990, the *Revue Historique des Armées* published a special issue on the French nuclear submarine programmes. In its pages, we learned in detail

3 July 1970 – a thermonuclear test on Mururoa. Named *Licorne*, this experimentation produced 914kt of energy, 75 times the power of the bomb dropped on Hiroshima. This image, both frightening and fascinating, has become emblematic of the nuclear age, along with the pictures of Hiroshima and Nagasaki, or the test in 1946 on the island of Bikini. The picture of the *Licorne* test is used by TV networks and other media around the world to illustrate a scenario of nuclear war in contemporary geopolitics. This picture was notably used to illustrate a programme by Russian TV after the annexation of Crimea. (CEA Photo)

about the hardships encountered in the development of propulsion of nuclear submarines, an obstacle overcome thanks to the indulgent cooperation of the US government in Washington.

In 1991, the above-mentioned French university group submitted its first thesis. Directed by Dominique Mongin, its title was *La genèse de l'armement atomique* (The Genesis of Atomic Weapons), which he later published in a book, *The French atomic bomb 1945–1958*. Historians were also interested in nuclear tests, which even made the subject of a symposium held on 12 June 1992. More academic works followed: *Essais nucléaires français*, a collective work published in 1996 by Bruyant; *Vers une marine atomiques* (Philippe Quérel, also published by Bruyant in 1997); and *Les moyens de la puissance: les activités militaires du CEA* (Jean-Damien Pô, published by Ellipses in 2001). Bertrand Goldschmidt, former director of the chemistry department at the Atomic Energy Commission (CEA), was also mobilised. He published *L'Aventure atomique* in 1962, *Les Rivalités atomiques* in 1967, *Le complexe atomique* in 1980 and *Les pionniers de l'atome* in 1987, this last being a book which faithfully reconstructed the French nuclear saga, from 1940's military trouncing to the first atomic tests in the Algerian Sahara. Jacques Vilain is also to be reckoned with. The former communications director of aerospace engine manufacturer Snecma wrote *La Force de dissuasion française. Genèse et évolution*, published in 1987 by Docavia/Larivière. Richly illustrated, the book is much sought after by collectors. In 2000, André Bendjebbar published a reference book, *L'Histoire secrète de la bombe atomique française* (The Secret History of the French Atomic Bomb). Its purpose highlights in particular France's early

nuclear research, led with regards to atomic weapons and nuclear energy just before the Second World War by Frédéric Joliot-Curie and his team at the *Collège de France*.

Bendjebbar's book also explains, out of modesty, how French politicians of the *IVe Republique* refused to allow the British to publish anything regarding the meticulous contribution of the French scientists, who had at that time sought protection in England, to the British nuclear works initiated by Winston Churchill under the secret 'Tube Alloy' programme. Publications increased in the 1990s at a steady pace as a result of the French Defence Department's desire for transparency. The French parliament has also been playing its public information role to the full by regularly publishing reports that address all subjects, including the most difficult. An internet website, accessible to the general public since 1995, has opened up new fields. Away from the institutions, the dark side is not ignored, particularly regarding the effects of nuclear testing, as in the book *Les Irradiés du Béryl* and other critical publications by Bruno Barrillot, himself a victim.

A question of Language

The much-welcomed transparency and willingness of Michèle Alliot-Marie, Jacques Chirac's Minister of Defence, who encouraged in the early days of the new millennium the publication of reports about the nuclear tests in the Algerian Sahara and then in the Pacific Islands, is also to be reckoned with. There is also the public report of the International Atomic Energy Agency, *Radiological situation on the atolls of Mururoa and Fangataufa*. Furthermore, the French

In January 1959, President Charles de Gaulle declared to the press: "We are in the atomic era and we are a country that can be destroyed at any moment, except if the aggressor is deterred from his undertaking by the certainty that he will, too, undergo terrible destruction." In 1959, in a speech at the *École Militaire* (Military Academy), he announced that France was going to have its *'Force de frappe'*. A veteran of the 1914–18 war, teacher of strategy at the *École de Guerre* (War Academy), brigadier general in the campaign of 1940 and chief of the Resistance, as president de Gaulle radically transformed the nation. By restoring an election regime in France, the *Ve Republique*, he created a special relationship between the citizens and their president, the one in charge of the nuclear fire. The notion of "nuclear monarchy" perfectly described this regime. (US Congress Library)

Henri Becquerel (15 December 1852 – 25 August 1908), a Nobel laureate, was the first to discover evidence of radioactivity. For his discovery, Henri Becquerel, along with Marie Skłodowska-Curie and her husband Pierre Curie, received the 1903 Nobel Prize in Physics. His name is used to designate the measure of radioactivity. Becquerel ushered a lineage of nuclear scientists, among them Albert Einstein, Ernest Rutherford (New Zealand, disintegration of the elements), James Chadwick (United Kingdom, discovery of the neutron), Max Planck (Germany, quantum mechanics), Enrico Fermi (Italy, nuclear reactions), Niels Bohr (Denmark, structure of the atom), Otto Hahn and Lise Meitner (Germany, nuclear fission), Ernest Lawrence (USA, discovery of plutonium), and in Russia, Abram Ioffe, Pyotr Kapista and Iakov Zeldovitch. (Smithsonian)

Intellectual works

The French nuclear technological edifice is therefore fully combined with a very well thought-out multidisciplinary intellectual construction, which is just as ambitious. The requirements are academic. As early as the 1950s, army colonel Charles Ailleret launched into this process with numerous articles in which he clarified the notion and added, with the support of General de Gaulle, the idea of an 'all-out' deterrent. Published in the *Revue de la Défense Nationale*, these articles were particularly influential on political decision-makers, in particular the leaders of the French parliament left-wing parties who took the decision against all odds to launch the development of the French atomic bomb, namely Prime Ministers Pierre Mendès-France and Guy Mollet.

The new *Ve Republique*, since 1958, had introduced a legal procedure at the highest level of the democratic sphere. The decisions were made at the Elysée Palace. The technical choices, formats and performances had conformed to their conclusions, the arbitrations being fixed by the French Defence Council under the presidency of the then French head of state. President René Coty (1954–59) planted the first seed, which was further grown and maintained by all the presidents of the French *Ve Republique*, beginning with Charles de Gaulle. It was, however, up to the Parliament to openly debate this very important issue. The intellectual construction of this new strategic order benefited from the creation of the Centre for Prospective and Evaluation at the Ministry of Defence from 1964 by its minister, Pierre Messmer. The works of the CPE defined the sufficient level of deterrence given to a nuclear force. The CEP adopted the notion of massive retaliation strikes at the strategic level, and the idea of "tests of the intentions of the adversary" by deploying nuclear tactical weapons in the scenario of a war in Europe. The CEP was backed from 1973 onwards by the Centre for Analysis and

parliament has published a number of reports on the *'Force de frappe'* nuclear deterrence force, a rich and valuable official source for perceiving the means of deterrence, which first of all is a clear political strategy.

Academic production has supported the national thinking on nuclear weapons. Following a public exhibition mounted by the *Service Historique de la Défense* in 2017 at the Château de Vincennes, a very meticulous book was published by the Odile Jacob publishing company, entitled *Résistance et Dissuasion. From the origins of the French nuclear programme to the present day*. Edited by Céline Jurgensen, a historian from the French *École Normale Supérieure*, and Dominique Mongin, certainly the most challenging academic in the country, this recent publication contributed towards the revival of French historiography. It demonstrated the involvement of former partisans acting against the German *Wehrmacht* who were, after the war, prominent decision-makers and managers of the French nuclear programme. The spirit of resistance and the culture of secret and indirect action were evident in their management culture and the engine of the philosophy "never again a war over France, never again occupation of the territory".

Unlike the United States and the United Kingdom, this history is the result of recent, almost contemporary works. In addition, all were in the very literary language of Jules Verne, making them difficult for English-speaking authors to access. Indeed, and because of that, contemporary books published in the USA or the UK only include brief information about French nuclear ambition. As such, the purpose of this book is to give a wider audience to a national adventure which is widely recognized as an incredible success.

An artist's vision of the air war during the First World War. This image took us back to the book *L'aviation militaire* of Clement Ader, published in 1908, which foresaw a deterrence role for strategic long-range bombers. (*Service Historique de la Défense*)

Marie Skodowska-Curie (7 November 1867 – 4 July 1934) was a pioneer of new science and member of the Solvay Conference. Her work in nuclear science has been applied in the medical domain. Born in Warsaw, she was the first woman to win a Nobel Prize, and the first and only to win the Nobel Prize in two scientific fields. She worked only on peaceful applications of her discoveries, diverging radically from any military purposes. Her legend was forged during the First World War by designing radiography vehicles, '*les Petites Curie*' (the Small Curie), thereby revolutionizing medicine. It was a mission she accomplished in one of these vehicles close to the front line in eastern France with her daughter, Irene. (Author's collection)

Forecasting (CAP) at the Ministry of Foreign Affairs. This non-elected body was an equivalent to the Policy Planning Staff of the US State Department. Animated by diplomats and academics, the CAP fed French university research, in particular along with the French IFRI think-tank which worked on the analysis of the perceived main threat, the Soviet Union.

The influence of Raymond Aron at the *Institut d'Études Politiques de Paris* should be mentioned. Inspired by the US vision of nuclear weapons – which was mostly anti-Soviet – he trained a whole generation of decision-makers and senior officials on the role of nuclear weapons in the defence of the Atlantic Alliance. As an editorial writer for the French conservative daily newspaper *Le*

Abram Ioffe, Marie Curie, Paul Langevin, Owen Willans Richardson, Lord Ernest Rutherford, Théophile de Donder, Maurice de Broglie, Louis de Broglie, Lise Meitner and James Chadwick. (Author's collection)

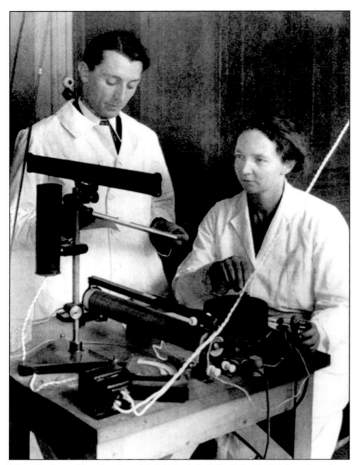

Irène Curie and her husband Frédéric Joliot-Curie in their laboratory in Paris, the building where they discovered artificial radioactivity in 1934. (CEA Photo)

Frédéric Joliot-Curie and his first circle, Hans von Halban and Lew Kowarski, at the *College de France*, the top-ranking academic institution of the country. In June 1940, their researchs on the atom bomb and nuclear energy was smuggled out of German-occupied France to England along with a supply of radium and heavy water. (CEA Photo)

Pierre Mendès-France, Prime Minister in 1954, decided, just after the defeat of Diem Bien Phu, to create a clandestine structure in the CEA to develop the atomic bomb. He fixed the organization of the works, entrusting the design of the nuclear charges to the CEA, and not to the laboratories of the armies, which however claimed the conduct of the project. The nuclear project was also a reaction after the arrival of Germany within NATO and its remilitarization. (*Photo Assemblée Nationale*)

Guy Mollet, Prime Minister in 1956. After the disaster of the Suez operation, he gave a decisive boost to the French nuclear programme with a budget increase and the launch of the Mirage IV project. Above all, he gave strong support to the defence of Israel and reconciled French socialism with two structuring subjects: free trade, by founding the European Common Market, and the atomic force. (*Archives nationales des Pays-Bas*)

Figaro, he had a great influence over a part of the national public opinion, then classified as the right and centre-left wing. We owe thanks to Captain Lars Wedim and *professeur* François Géré for having clearly synthesized this edifice in their books *Marianne et Athéna* and *La Pensée stratégique française contemporaine* (Éditions Economica).

One reference book remains – *Nuclear Strategies*. Written in 1977 by General Lucien Poirier, this pedagogy of the atom bomb, with high density of style, full of philosophic notions, requires careful reading. We can remember this sentence: "The notion of credibility is the pivot of the dissuasive reasoning of the adversary and of the strategic calculation of nuclear strategies." To dissuade is first to convince, Poirier explains. Deterrence certainly works only if it is nuclear, according to a complex calculation that involves risks and benefits. A deep continuity can also be observed in the institutions of the French *Ve Republique*, which has all the features of an elective nuclear monarchy by weaving a quasi-divine link between the president and the country via direct universal suffrage. Since then, changes in doctrine have occurred only at the margins.

Later on, tactical nuclear weapons deployed to halt a land-based aggression were reclassified as pre-strategic, at the request of President François Mitterrand. Even if they are aimed at opposing forces, their purpose is to show determination and restore deterrence through a potential exercise of limited strikes. Then

RÉPUBLIQUE FRANÇAISE

MINISTÈRE
DE L'INDUSTRIE ET DU COMMERCE

SERVICE
de la PROPRIÉTÉ INDUSTRIELLE

BREVET D'INVENTION

Gr. 14. — Cl. 3.

N° 971.324

Perfectionnements aux charges explosives.

CAISSE NATIONALE DE LA RECHERCHE SCIENTIFIQUE résidant en France (Seine).

Demandé le 4 mai 1939, à 15ʰ 35ᵐ, à Paris.
Délivré le 12 juillet 1950. — Publié le 16 janvier 1951.

(Brevet d'invention dont la délivrance a été ajournée en exécution de l'article 11, § 7,
de la loi du 5 juillet 1844 modifiée par la loi du 7 avril 1902.)

On sait que l'absorption d'un neutron par un noyau d'uranium peut provoquer la rupture de ce dernier avec dégagement d'énergie et émission de nouveaux neutrons en nombre en moyenne supérieur à l'unité. Parmi les neutrons ainsi émis, un certain nombre peuvent à leur tour provoquer sur des noyaux d'uranium, de nouvelles ruptures, et les ruptures de noyaux d'uranium pourront ainsi aller en croissant suivant une progression géométrique, avec dégagement de quantités extrêmement considérables d'énergie. Ces chaînes de ruptures successives peuvent se ramifier d'une manière illimitée, et la réaction peut devenir explosive.

On a cherché, conformément à la présente invention, à rendre pratiquement utilisable cette réaction explosive, non seulement pour des travaux de mine et pour des travaux publics, mais encore pour la constitution d'engins de guerre, et d'une manière très générale dans tous les cas où une force explosive est nécessaire.

Or, pour rendre cette utilisation pratique, il faut se reporter à la notion de masse ou en général de conditions critiques dont il a déjà été fait mention dans la demande de brevet français du 1ᵉʳ mai 1939 pour « Dispositif de production d'énergie ».

Il existe en effet, toutes choses égales d'ailleurs, une valeur critique de la masse d'uranium au-dessous de laquelle la ramification des chaînes cesse d'être illimitée. Et l'on a déjà indiqué dans cette demande de brevet que l'on pouvait, avec les données actuelles de la science, estimer, par des expériences progressives, la valeur de la masse critique.

On peut aussi évaluer cette masse critique M pour un composé ou un mélange homogène d'uranium (ne contenant pas d'hydrogène)

en utilisant la formule suivante, valable pour une masse sphérique :

$$M = \frac{4}{3} \times \pi^4 \left[3\,D\,(n\,P - A) \right]^{-\frac{3}{2}}$$

dans laquelle :

D est la somme, pour tous les corps simples présents dans la masse, des produits de la concentration (en nombre d'atomes par cm³) par la section efficace des noyaux pour la diffusion des neutrons rapides,

A est la somme analogue, dans laquelle les sections efficaces de diffusion sont remplacées par les sections efficaces d'absorption,

P est le produit de la concentration de l'uranium (en nombre d'atomes par cm³) par la section efficace, pour le phénomène de partition, du noyau d'uranium vis-à-vis des neutrons rapides,

n. est le nombre moyen de neutrons émis lors d'une partition nucléaire de l'uranium.

Cette formule donne, à titre d'exemple, une masse critique de quelques dizaines de tonnes pour de l'oxyde d'uranium en poudre; et de quelques tonnes pour de l'uranium métallique.

On a montré également, dans la demande de brevet français précitée, comment cette masse critique pouvait être diminuée : soit en disposant autour de la masse des corps diffusants, (fer, plomb ou autres) en couche plus ou moins épaisse, et formant par exemple une enveloppe complète ou partielle autour de la masse (une enveloppe en fer de quelques dizaines de centimètres d'épaisseur réduisant par exemple la masse critique au tiers environ de sa valeur dans le cas de l'oxyde d'uranium en poudre); soit en accroissant la densité de la substance qui constitue la masse (la masse critique étant proportionnelle à l'inverse du carré de la densité).

0 – 00864

Prix du fascicule : 25 francs.

The patent for the atomic bomb, document number 971-324, registered on 4 May 1939 by Frédéric Joliot-Curie, Hans Halban and Lew Kowarski at the *Caisse nationale de la recherche scientifique* (National scientific research bank). The document was hidden during the German occupation of France. The patent fell into the public domain in 1959. (CEA Photo)

operational stance, in which the Rafale-launched awe-inspiring weapon is also calibrated for a strategic response. This has been demonstrated during the French Air Force's annual series of 'Poker' large scale FAS training and demonstration operations, which obviously also spares the nuclear submarine(s) on patrol of their dedicated 'second strike' retaliation capacity.

Sovereign and united: the French bomb today as in the past, a factor of peace

In 1973, at NATO's Ottawa summit, the final declaration recognised the French strike force's contribution to the security of the Atlantic Alliance, on par with the American and British nuclear forces. This was distinctly a consecration delivered to France by Washington. Indeed, the French deterrence strategy had the effect of complicating the war calculations of the main adversary – the Soviet Union – under the claimed strategy of 'the weak to the strong'. By 1974, as the Cold War went on, France had a buried strategic missile base and three nuclear-powered ballistic missile submarines (SSBNs) capable of going to sea at any time. This fleet, which made up the Strategic Oceanic Force, was increased to a total of five vessels at the end of the 1970s, then six in 1985.

Half a century later, our contemporary world is neither peaceful nor humanistic, and quite far from being democratic everywhere. France – as the historical cradle of the 18th-century Enlightenment – has an exorbitant privilege of having the right, in the legal

President Jacques Chirac, in a speech delivered in June 2001 at the Military School of Paris, mentioned the possibility of striking political targets, even with precise conventional weapons, besides demographic targets, which was the initial option of the nuclear strategy. President François Hollande recalled this point in his speech about French deterrence in February 2016. This mission is carried out today by the Rafale-launched ASMP-A missiles. President of the Republic since 2017, Émmanuel Macron has confirmed this very

sense, to possess the 'supreme weapon'; a right granted by the Non-Proliferation Treaty. This right, as defined by Article 51 of its Charter, is recognised by the United Nations and by a court judgment of the International Court of Justice. As a permanent member of the UN Security Council with the right to veto any of the Council's decision, France shares this competence with the four other nuclear powers recognised by the treaty (United States, Russia, China and the United Kingdom).

General director of the CEA, Pierre Guillaumat, was the manager of the nation's nuclear ambition in the 1950s. A Gaullist and former member of the Resistance, he embodied the continuity in the project through political change. Graduating from *École Polytechnique*, the military academy which formed the 'Elite of the Nation', he was one of the high-ranking civil servants who rebuilt the nation after the war. At the head of the CEA, he secretly selected the best scientists to build the teams for the 'Bomb' far before the official decision to launch atomic military applications. He was Minister of Defence for President de Gaulle, then Minister of Scientific Research. (Author's collection)

General (formerly Colonel) Charles Ailleret, who played a crucial role in explaining through books and articles the advantages of nuclear forces for a new defence policy in the nuclear age. During the 1950s, he demonstrated that a nuclear programme was within the financial capability of a country like France, adding to his message the diplomatic and military benefits of such weapons. (Author's collection)

It is hard to imagine today that Paris could decide to give up its nuclear deterrent. French diplomacy therefore has the possibility of exploiting this asset to encourage the process of combating proliferation. It is also provided with a relative 'freedom of action' in distant peace-making operations, alone or with its allies. The economic constraint, by definition cyclical, cannot serve the anti-nuclear option: each year, the country's Gross Domestic Product exceeds that of the previous year. France's present defence budget, representing 1.85 percent of its GDP, is considered still bearable. Unilateral disarmament is ruled out: the disappearance of the French nuclear arsenal would create an unprecedented situation of imbalance in Europe; even more so since Brexit. As nature abhors vacuum, a French retreat would be quickly exploited in the West by the United States and other Europeans, and in the East by the Russian Federation. France's status as a permanent member of the UN Security Council would quickly become an ejection seat. On a continent under pressure and threats, French deterrence makes even more sense nowadays. In matters of diplomacy, it is said one only lends to the rich. On the other hand, withdrawing behind neutrality, necessarily illusory, is not an option. When France left the integrated command of NATO in 1966, under de Gaulle's direction, the move did not change anything in terms of Atlantic solidarity, in application of Article 5, which establishes the principle of collective security and therefore solidarity with European and American allies.

Cooperation with the USA continued: this book will return to the American contribution to our nuclear strike force, something well beyond the purchase of Boeing KC-135 tankers. Moreover, the French defence industry was then being mobilised in close European industrial cooperation: i.e. the Jaguar fighter and the Martel air-to-ground missile with the British. Let us also mention mine warfare with Belgium and the Netherlands.

There was even the idea at the end of the 1980s of designing a joint air-to-ground nuclear missile with the United Kingdom. As François Mitterrand bluntly told his counterparts at a summit: "France is not on the planet Mars." This line of solidarity, independence and sovereignty was reaffirmed by the 2017 Strategic Review signed by President Émmanuel Macron, and it has remained unchanged since the first White Paper on Defence of 1972, written under President Georges Pompidou. Evidently, this perennial solution cannot rest nowadays on the European project alone: it is bogged down as the

Marcel Dassault in front of his Mystère IV. The aircraft's capabilities had been evaluated by Charles 'Chuck' Yeager in December 1952 in a mission to select a European fighter for off-shore orders to equip NATO forces. On its 34th flight, on 17 January 1953, it broke the sound barrier. He recruited the best engineers graduating from high schools and made the most rational technical options in close cooperation with the air force command. (Dassault Aviation)

This image is the symbol of a special strategic relationship. As Winston Churchill said, blending humour and admiration, General de Gaulle was dressed in the same uniform as the 'Unknown soldier', a joke in reference to the unknown private buried under the *Arc de Triomphe* in Paris. Churchill's vision for the future hierarchy of power was to restore the position of France in Europe, creating a balanced situation on the continent. (Author's collection)

President Charles de Gaulle, in the uniform of a general for an inspection visit at Istres Air Base, meeting the crews of Mirage IVs. The nuclear programme represented his main achievements, among other modernization projects of the nation: freeways, rapid trains, Concorde, the electronics industry, telecommunications networks and even ski resorts. (*Armée de l'Air Photo*)

Le Redoubtable in the arsenal of Cherbourg in Normandy. It was the first of a class of five submarines planned by the law programme of 1960. The nuclear-powered sub was loaded with 16 ballistic missiles, giving the strongest credibility to the French nuclear retaliation force. In the wake of its first operational patrols in 1972, NATO officially admitted at the Ottawa summit the contribution of France to the defence of the Alliance. (Naval Group)

EU sourly mobilises on its internal fractures. The then president of the National Assembly's defence committee, Mrs Patricia Adam, MP for the Brittany region of France, wrote in June 2014: "What makes France's rank is deterrence. It gives our country the capacity to respond alone to a vital threat; a vital threat that we can only define ourselves." French defence, she insisted, was therefore based on "the combination of traditional deterrence – force projection – and nuclear deterrence."

Enhanced legitimacy

It is clear that the present world is set to remain permanently nuclear. One can deplore this, but one cannot ignore the realities of human nature. In the past, brilliant civilizations have succumbed to totalitarianism in order to engage in organized slaughter: Adolf Hitler's Third Reich, Stalin's Soviet Union, Mao's Chinese People's Republic. On the territories its imperial armies had

A Mirage IV, the first carrier of the French nuclear strategy. Entrusted to the Dassault design office, this supersonic aircraft was created in 1956 under the social-democratic administration of Guy Mollet, then became the first weapon of the nuclear strike force of General de Gaulle. At the time, no aircraft had been designed to cruise at Mach 2 for a long period of time. Work on the aircraft was reused to develop Concorde in cooperation with British engineers. The ribbon for the speed record is clearly visible on the Mirage's fuselage. (Author's collection)

conquered, Japan massacred: Chinese, Koreans, prisoners of war, even the French citizens of Indochina. One could be extremely cultured and still prefer dictatorship to democracy. On the other hand, the atom bomb's message was understandable to all. It was more than a 'red line'. Would the French people agree to concede the military power of the atom to others, even friendly allies or brittle alliances? This force indeed contributed to France's credibility when it defended its own national values in front of other powers, not all of which were motivated by humanism and human rights.

The French nuclear deterrent tool is often presented as the country's life insurance, a choice made by a population where public discourse is more or less open to all. The French

The S2 nuclear missile, from the *Plateau d'Albion* nuclear base in south-east France, was displayed to the public during a military parade for Bastille Day. The adhesion of the population to the '*Force de frappe*' has regularly increased, recent opinion polls suggesting over 80 percent in favour of the nuclear deterrent. (*Photo Ministère de la defense*)

President François Mitterrand with Ronald Reagan in the 1980s. The socialist president contributed to forging the political consensus between the left and right wings necessary for the solidity of France's nuclear ambitions. (US DoD)

A famous book by Raymond Aron, leading French academic in geopolitics. He informed generations of law and politics students about defence issues during the 1960s and 1970s at the *Institut d'édudes politiques de Paris*. Aron's position was in line with Robert McNamara, President John F. Kennedy's Secretary of Defense, who was opposed to independent nuclear forces inside NATO, considering it "dangerous, expensive, prone to obsolescence and lacking in credibility". The NATO declaration at Ottawa radically denied this position. Aron was also a very active militant opposed to communist regimes. (Author's collection)

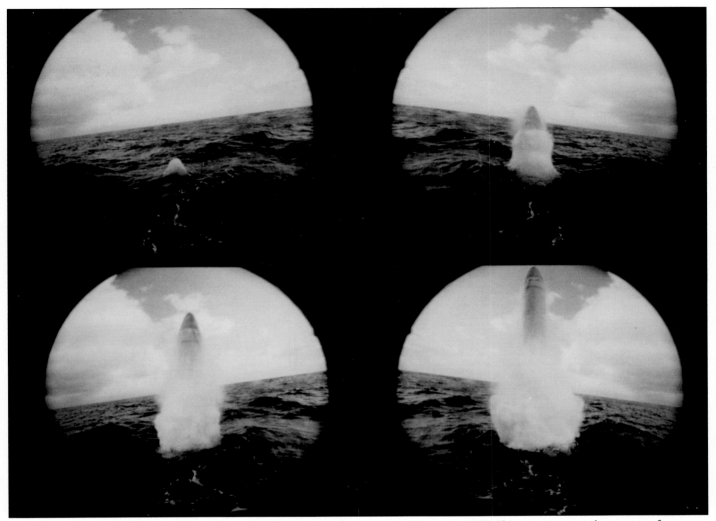

The launch of a M4 ballistic missile achieved by the *Force océanique stratégique*, or FOST. This asset was at the centre of a retaliation concept and the core of the deterrence strategy with nuclear weapons. The French concept was close to the strategy designed by the United States and Great Britain. (Arian Groupe)

concept is all the more relevant as its elaboration has benefited from the freedom of thought and debate that only a democratic country knows how to grant, an intellectual exercise that has not ceased since the first critical considerations of Nobel Prize winner and French writer Albert Camus at the announcement of the Hiroshima bombing on 6 August 1945.

Journalists and sociologists are fully committed to this topic. The French government is far from being ignorant about that and needs to expose the merits of its strategy. This is the mission of the *Institut des Hautes Etudes de Défense Nationale*, which arranges annually academic sessions about nuclear deterrence for the country's executives: parliamentarians, leaders of big companies or small business, churchmen and journalists. Your servant was able to take advantage of these privileged times, which take a happy few to a strategic submarine, an air base or an aircraft-carrier. Everyone, every citizen, can observe today the relics of this epic that museums have put in majesty: at Le Bourget, at Cherbourg, at Caen. A short chapter will have the look of a touristic guide. Detached from its technological aspects, the field of reflection has invaded the philosophical field. This is also the strength of the French nuclear strategy: a well-informed debate on deterrence which, in the end, has consolidated its foundations. Opinion polls are revealing. Supported by only a small majority in the 1960s, France's strategy and its nuclear strike force were accepted, 60 years later, by more than 80 percent of those questioned in 2022.

A focus on the sequence 1930– 90: the building of the strategic triad

This first volume of this work will plunge us into the early works of the 1930s and the nuclear imperative which imposed itself on post-war France, from 1945, with its multiple military and political contributions. The 'Force de frappe' mobilized the best part of French industry and science from 1945. From 1958 onwards, General de Gaulle gave a new impulse: the 'Force de frappe' should not only re-establish France's position within the Atlantic Alliance, but also serve a posture of independence and carry a strong international message, a certain idea of the world that many would like to be more humanistic, more UN-like. In the service of this strategy, the atomic force is steered by the Delegation of Armaments in the Ministry of Defence (DMA), the design of the weapons being entrusted to the Atomic Energy Commission (CEA). The DMA and CEA have a mission of organization of the programme while carrying out a contractor capacity through industry and the private sector.

This national project is characterized by a continuity that transcends political changes and results in a French strategic triad composed of nuclear ballistic missile submarines, silo-based surface-to-surface missiles and a long-range strategic strike air force equipped with Mirage IV supersonic bombers. Integrated with conventional forces, a tactical force is also constituted with mobile ground-to-ground missiles, Mirage III and Jaguar fighter-bombers and flotillas of Super Étendard fighter-bombers on aircraft carriers.

This force has been constantly modernized in order to guarantee its credibility. The warheads were also perfected by the CEA: the A-bomb in 1960, the H-bomb in 1968 and neutron warheads in the late 1970s. From a sociological and cultural point of view, this ambition has largely transcended the sole objective of defence in the face of the threat of the Cold War, to the point that historians have come to believe that the atom bomb is now part of the French nation's DNA.

The king's last word

Nuclear deterrence, in France's view, is at the heart of an existential paradox that has remained unchanged since the 1960s. This paradox is best expressed by the official insignia of the *Forces aériennes stratégiques*, a sword held frozen in its sheath grasped by a steel gauntlet, whose heraldry is inspired by none other than the knights of the Middle Ages, therefore setting the whole '*Force de frappe*' in a thousand-year-old martial history. The motto inscribed by Louis XIV on his armies' cannons was 'The king's last word', and each of the monarch's guns had its own awe inspiring name: *Redoutable,*

Inflexible, Tonnant – the names given to the first French SSBNs. This sovereign nuclear weapon extends around France a space of military security and invites partnership and negotiation. Since 1964, when the Mirage IV entered service, the country has been a sanctuary, while this posture is a commitment to the allies' cause. This solidarity comes under the collective security provided for by NATO (Article 5) and Article 42 of the European Union. Since February 2022, the war in Ukraine has consolidated the legitimacy of deterrence.

The second volume of this work will be focused on the post-Cold War period and preparation for the future. The horizon is today the year 2100. This second volume will have specific categories on new-generation submarines, new intercontinental ballistic missiles, the nuclear aircraft carriers and Rafale aircraft, new weapons and the nuclear simulation programme. The new-generation force is led by two mandatory specifications: technological parity, sufficient in terms of strike capacity, and henceforth all-azimuths.

In France, the concept is so strong that the word 'deterrence' could be translated as 'nuclear'. Deterrence means nuclear and vice versa. The two words are totally fused *en Français.*

1
FROM BOMB A TO BOMB H

In the early hours of Saturday, 13 February 1960, a telephone rang in the Paris office of the French Minister of the Armies.

"So what Messmer?"

At the other end of the line, one could hear the general's strong, deep and somewhat worried voice.

The minister replied: "Everything went very well General."

There was a silence, but then came the general's stinging reply to Pierre Messmer: "A little more, I could have learned that from the radio."

More than 2,500 miles from Paris, in the sands of the Algerian desert, the first French atomic bomb had just exploded at 7:04 a.m. A moment later, at 7:05 a.m., the Minister of the Armies received a telegram informing him of the success of *Gerboise bleue*, the name of the operation that until then had been kept secret. The name chosen was a small Saharan desert mammal which moves by leaps and bounds with its long hind legs.

Designed by the CEA, the infernal experiment machine was fired in a forlorn and inhabited area in Reggane in southern Algeria, then a French territory. The device was a plutonium bomb that had been placed on top of a 300ft-high metal tower. To observe the phenomenon, engineers had placed measuring instruments and high-speed cameras all around it. The military, for their part, had set up decommissioned tanks and aircraft on the scene so as to observe the result of the explosion on war materiel. The device released 40 kilotons of energy, three times the power of the Hiroshima bomb. At that time, the military atom bomb was still the exclusive domain of the United States, Russia and the United Kingdom. France was now part of the 'club of four', later joined by China, which was to demonstrate its nuclear capacity only in October 1964. The French

February 1960 explosion was a grandiose moment, signifying the return of France on the international scene.

At 7:46 a.m., French President Charles de Gaulle wrote: "Hurrah for France! Since this morning, the country is stronger and prouder. From the bottom of my heart, I thank all who have achieved this magnificent success for France." For this man of letters with a refined vocabulary, the football match-style words may come as a surprise. But they were well chosen and inspired by popular language; the general's onomatopoeia can be understood anywhere, in any language and by anyone. This congratulatory telegram (today it would have been a tweet) was addressed to Pierre Guillaumat, then the Delegate for Atomic Energy to the Prime Minister.

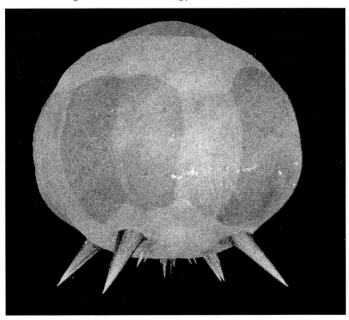

Gerboise bleue was the name of the first French nuclear device, which was detionated on 13 February 1960 at 7:04 a.m. and produced 40 kilotons of energy. (CEA Photo)

IVe Republique: the fight between supporters and opponents of nuclear weapons

As early as 1945, everything necessary to start a military nuclear programme in France was legally in place. The creation of the *Commissariat à l'énergie atomique* (CEA) on 18 October 1945 took the form of an ordinance signed by General de Gaulle, then president of the council of the French provisional government (GPRF). Article 1 of its founding statutes states that the CEA "shall pursue scientific and technical research with a view to the use of atomic energy in the various fields of science, industry and national defence". You read 'national defence' correctly, as this was nothing more than a military ambition. Defence, in short, can therefore mean nuclear reactors for combat ships or an atomic bomb.

The French political class and the CEA's leaders were very divided about the idea of designing a nuclear weapon. However, the massive use of nuclear science in electricity and medicine for the reconstruction of France provided a formidable consensus across the whole political spectrum. The debate on the military use of the atom bomb was launched in a country where the French Communist Party (PCF), following Stalin's orders to the letter, represented 20–25 percent of the national vote. Beyond the scores of seats obtained in the post-war legislative elections, the PCF likewise had a strong influence in intellectual circles.

However, the ideas of General de Gaulle and his supporters in favour of designing nuclear weapons were soon to find support from the governing French socialist party, thanks to the ongoing planetary geopolitical events. They had to fight against the communists, but also against the centrists, who, from 1955 onwards, were strongly supporting a European common defence, even possibly wielding nuclear weapons that they dreamt of developing and sharing with Germany and Italy. The arrival in power of General de Gaulle, however, clearly put an end to any European 'colouring' of nuclear weapons. It was therefore the sovereign French approach that would prevail, all the more easily since a nuclear strategy can only be national when it concerns the defence of a nation's vital interests.

Three vicious traumas experienced during the 1950s – when the French socialists were in governmental power – led to its rallying to the atomic military option. In 1955, the bitter defeat of Dien Bien Phu in Indochina convinced Prime Minister Pierre Mendès-France to launch the first French endeavour in developing nuclear weapons within the CEA. It was above all a way of erasing the psychological humiliation of the Indochinese defeat, especially since the Soviet film-maker Roman Karmen had orchestrated the staging of thousands of French prisoners in the news. The French leaders also knew that US President Eisenhower had finally cancelled Operation *Vultur*, a nuclear raid planned on Ho Chi Minh's troops in order to help the besieged French soldiers. At the end of 1955, Mendès-France asked the CEA to create the *Bureau des Études Générales*, a clandestine department in charge of the first research efforts regarding the new weapon.

Then came the rearmament issue of Germany, a process that began the same year. It is true that the new *Bundeswehr* would be placed under the supervision of NATO, but France wanted to boast of being a member of the Alliance with a superior status, a status that required

This mushroom of *Gerboise bleue* was photographed by a Vautour aircraft. *Gerboise bleue* had a core of plutonium integrated at the centre of the implosion. Scientists then had to work on its miniaturization to integrate the explosive in an operational weapon. (CEA Photo)

Marcoule nuclear plant, south of the area between Lyon and Marseilles, where the plutonium for the first French nuclear bombs was produced. At the height of the military activities of the CEA, its manpower reached 8,200 people. (CEA Photo)

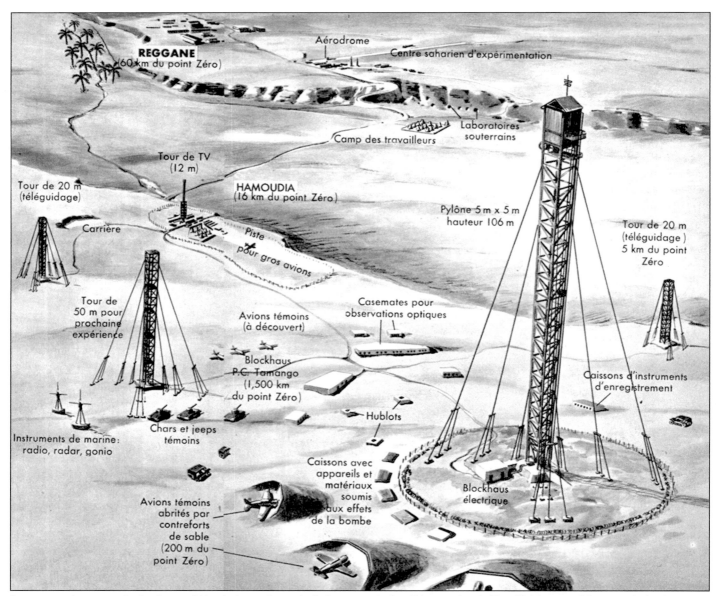

Reggane nuclear range, in the desert of Algeria, is a real town built from scratch. Conditions are harsh. The official name of the range is the *Centre Saharien d'Expérimentation Militaire* (CSEM). French Prime Minister Guy Mollet gave the go-ahead for its construction on 10 May 1957. Protected by the army, this military establishment had a surface of 108,000km². Unlike with their American colleagues at the Nevada tests site, who were close to Las Vegas, personnel at Regane had no entertainment in the vicinity. Attempts were made to build a swimming pool, but lack of water meant it was impossible to fill. The site was linked to the outside world by a 2.4km aviation runway. (CEA Photo)

nothing other than the crossing of a military threshold: the possession of the atomic bomb. The diplomatic humiliation of Suez in 1956, combined with the threat of Soviet reprisals and the implicit condemnation of Eisenhower's Washington, was too much for France. Guy Mollet, then President of the French socialist council, rallied to the 'bomb' and also initiated the ambitious Mirage IV bomber programme. Thus, the vicious defeat of 1940, that of Dien Bien Phu in 1955 and finally the failure of Suez in 1956 accelerated the decision-making process. Moreover, the

Military equipment, uniforms, vehicles and aircraft were posted near point zero to observe the effects of an atomic explosion, as had happened at the Nevada test range. (CEA Photo)

The experimental atomic device on top of a 100m-tall metal tower. From Reggane, a 45km road leads to the Advanced Command Post, from where the order was given to trigger the bomb, located at Point Zero, 14km away. The four atmospheric tests here were followed by tests in an underground gallery at a new experimental site, the Centre for Military Oasis Experiments (CEMO). This second range was established in the Hoggar massif, near In Ekker, 150km to the north of Tamanrasset. (CEA Photo)

inter-allied European environment – in this case a way of finding military and political parity with the United Kingdom – plus German rearmament invited Paris to aspire to a nuclear status.

First: a clandestine programme

Pierre Guillaumat is one of those energetic senior French officials who led to the bomb's creatrion. A former Resistance fighter, he had graduated from the *École Polytechnique*, a competitive school that trains military engineers – the elite of the nation, as the popular

saying goes. Appointed administrator of the CEA, a position he held throughout the 1950s, he was a supporter of General de Gaulle and discarded the pacifist ideology that prevailed at the CEA in the wake of his predecessor, Frédéric Joliot-Curie. Guillaumat was the architect of the French bomb in its scientific and economic dimensions, creating a direct link between science and industry. His philosophy was to put pure research at rest, and instead to put theory into practice. With the support of many French politicians, he turned the CEA into an industrial establishment. The laboratory spadework continued, but found its application in the first nuclear power plant built at Marcoule, on the Rhône, between Lyon and Marseille.

This plant was given the task of producing the plutonium necessary for the first 'bomb'. It took only four years for French scientists and engineers to move from theory to experimentation. Within the French armed forces, the commander of a special weapons unit was clandestinely installed and prepared the construction of a test range in the southern Algerian desert. It was at this stage that Colonel Charles Ailleret, a theorist of nuclear strategy, intervened. His organisation – the Special Weapons Section – was inspired by the US Nevada Test Site and took advantage of the unerring report he had authored. As an officer of a NATO allied country, he had had the privilege to be a guest of the American authorities to attend the US site to witness an atomic explosion.

The technological option was identical to that adopted for the Nagasaki bomb: a centripetal implosion, with the plutonium modules arranged in a sphere and the conventional explosive distributed around the periphery. As a specialised corps in explosives, the DEFA laboratory of the French Army intervened for the mechanical part of the process, that which would violently gather the plutonium. *Gerboise bleue* was an experimental device, so it was up to the French design offices to make it an operational weapon. Three further tests were conducted at the Reggane site, while 13 more, underground this time, were supervised on the In Ain Ekker range. These experiments made it possible to validate

A *Breguet Deux-Ponts* of the French Air Force. With a range of 4,000 km, the aircraft was used to transport personnel and equipment, notably the nuclear components of the bomb. Three of these aircraft were acquired by the French administration. These and the six Sahara aircraft acquired from Air France provided the *Armée de l'air* with a valuable transport fleet for moving personnel and materials to the Pacific test range. The Sahara fleet was retired in 1972. (*Armée de l'Air*)

In the French daily newspapers, the experiment was hailed as a victory, as seen in the headlines of this Parisian paper. The international press was more circumspect, even critical. (CEA Photo)

law that set the formation of the 'Force de frappe', Prime Minister Michel Debré had to commit his responsibility before the deputies for the vote on the text. At the instigation of General de Gaulle, the funds allocated to atomic research were multiplied by seven between 1959 and 1963. According to opinion polls in 1959, 38 percent were in favour of a national atomic weapon, with opponents representing 37 percent. In 1968, when the Mirage IV became an operational reality, the supporters still only obtained 43 percent. The balance of power changed again in 1969 following the departure from power of de Gaulle. Signalling his rallying, François Mitterrand, his socialist opponent and future applicant for presidential polls, declared: "I said during my 1965 presidential campaign that I would ban the strike force. I will not be able to say it again elsewhere. General de Gaulle's military policy was approved by the French […] Soon our atomic armament will be an irreversible reality." The criticism did not only come from the left, but also from pro-European centrist lukewarm circles. In the context of the Cold War and ideological war, Raymond Aron, in his book *Le Grand débat – Initiation à la stratégie atomique*, produced this astonishing sentence: "There is a fundamental difference between possessing a few atomic and thermonuclear

the AN-11 and AN-22 free-fall nuclear weapons and allow for the organisation of the very first Mirage IV squadrons.

The 'Force de frappe', in search of a political consensus

Resistance to the French bomb was always mingled with political opposition to General de Gaulle. The historian André Bendjebbar notes in his book *Histoire secrète de la bombe atomique française* that the press, both national and international, was rather critical when the test was announced. The tone was even akin to persiflage. Newspapers and French people in the street bantered about a 'bombinette' to describe the 'Force de frappe'. Incidentally, this very word makes it seem more acceptable, even sympathetic. In France, we like small things.

Decisions were anyway taken away from the *cafés*, politics, congresses and editorial offices. In order to adopt the procurement

bombs, as well as a few bombers, and having a deterrent force." This is a direct attack on the principle of equalizing other powers' advantage through having nuclear bombs too, the founding principle of the French strategy of deterrence. In 1981, when François Mitterrand arrived at the Elysée Palace, deterrence already had received 67 percent support, then 72 percent in 1985. The shift in opinion was clear. During the Cold War, we can remember the support of public opinion for the firm position expressed by François Mitterrand in 1982 in front of the members of the German *Bundestag*, "The pacifists are in the West and the missiles are in the East", in reference to the SS20 missiles. However, Nena's pop hit '99 *Luftballons*' was playing over and over again on the radio. The favourable opinion was now between 80 and 90 percent in favour, which cannot be compatible with a desire to disarm in the French public opinion.

Thermonuclear objective: the 'general' is turning impatient

Once the A-bomb was mastered, the next milestone for France was to go thermonuclear. For high-powered explosions, it was necessary to leave southern Algeria, especially since independence for the former colony had been signed in Evian in 1962. Thermonuclear technology pushed the French teams to the Pacific atolls in Polynesia.

While the A-bomb was developed *ab initio* in less than four years, the French formula adopted in order to obtain atomic fusion did not work at all. Great effort were made in consuming a large budget, in particular for the production of military uranium and the conduct of tests, but without achieving the expected result.

The 'general' was not happy. The idea of a 'boosted' A-bomb instead was far from meeting his requirements. The H-bomb is as much a military ambition as a political one. The Gaullist epic had a fusional relationship with technology. Renunciation was not an option. In January 1966, de Gaulle was said to have declared to Alain Peyrefitte, then his Minister of Research:

> Find out why the Atomic Energy Commission cannot manage to make the H-bomb. It's interminable! I have just been told that it will take many more years. I can't wait more than two or three years! I will not finish this seven-year term. I had to run for office, to make sure of it. But I won't go all the way. Only, before I leave, I want the first experiment to have taken place! Are we going to be, of the five nuclear powers, the only one that will not reach the thermonuclear level? Are we going to let the Chinese overtake us? If we don't get there while I'm here, we'll never get there.

The rest of his quote remains very topical: "My successors, whether they are on one side or the other, will not dare to brave the shouting of the Anglo-Americans, the Communists, the old maids and the priests. But if a first explosion has taken place, my successors will not dare to stop the development of such weapons."

In London, the intervention of General Thoulouze

On 27 January 1967, General de Gaulle went to the Limeil-Brévane CEA centre. The schedule that was presented to him mentioned a first thermonuclear test planned for 1970. The general reacted badly, urging the departure of Pierre Billaud, the CEA director. To better understand the crisis then going on at the CEA, one can consult the memoirs of Raoul Dautray recorded in his autobiography *Du Vel D'hiv à la bombe H*. His birth name had been Ignace Robert Kouchelevitz, but the Kouchelevitz family did not escape the roundups carried out against the Jews in France in 1942 with the active complicity of *Maréchal* Pétain's Vichy regime. Ignace owed his miraculous

An AN-22 under the fuselage of a Mirage IVA. The AN-22 free-fall nuclear bomb type could produce a yield of 60 kilotons. The concept of this plutonium bomb was similar to the design of the bomb at Nagasaki, with a sphere of fission metal at the centre. Dassault Aviation was part of the development regarding the aerodynamics of the bomb and connectivity between the aircraft and the weapon. (Photo by author)

The Canopus experiment on 24 August 1968 demonstrated the thermonuclear capability of the *'Force de frappe'*. The test produced 2.6 megatons of energy over Fangataufa atoll. Two weeks later, on 8 September, the Procion test on Mururoa confirmed the new thermonuclear status of France, the bomb yielding 1.28 megatons. (CEA Photo)

The S3D ballistic missile armed with a 1 megaton re-entry vehicle. A similar payload was integrated on the M20 missile of the Redoutable-class submarine. (Photo Aerospatiale/ArianeGroup)

salvation to a former minister and railway engineer, Raoul Dautray, who hid him and gave him shelter in his country house for the rest of the war. The young student was tremendously gifted in science, after the war passing all the competitive examinations for the best engineering schools. He attended *Polytechnique*, where he achieved the second-best marks in his class in 1949. It was at this time that the new CEA spotted him and recruited his burgeoning talent. There, he was assigned to the theoretical physics team of Jules Horowitz, a survivor of the camps. Robert Dautray succeeded in developing the right formula, but his efforts were rejected in favour of others.

After a disappointing 1967 firing campaign in the Pacific, the young scientist returned to work. The research teams were reorganized and Dautray finally managed to have his formula developed. To speed things up, the CEA teams decided to have their equations validated by the British. It should be noted that France had left the integrated command of NATO a year earlier, yet London still welcomed the French in a friendly manner. A mission was led by General Thoulouze, the French military *attaché* in London. While the A-bomb is a problem of physics and mechanics, the phenomenon of fusion is above all, according to Dautray, a mathematical issue. With his scheme requiring validation, to make up for lost time and save budgets, Dautray wrote down a series of questions to be presented to the British atomists at Aldermaston. The British warned that they would not be able to give away any data, nor any plan or formula, but agreed to answer each question with a 'yes' or 'no'. The CEA-DAM (the military applications arm of the French Atomic Energy Division) went back to work on new bases, the work of a second team led by Michel Carayol – whose calculations had been validated by Sir William Cook, the father of the British H-bomb – being sanctioned by the Canopus test on 24

August 1968 on Fangataufa atoll at the *Centre d'Expérimentations du Pacifique* (Pacific Experimental Centre, or CEP). At some 1,500ft off the ground under a balloon, the first French H-bomb test released 2.6 megatons (more than 100 times the power of the Nagasaki weapon). Its success was confirmed by a second test on 8 September that year that produced 1.28 megatons.

There are no records to confirm this, but Paris is said to have returned the favour for the help of the British atomists by agreeing to lift its veto on the UK's entry into the European Economic Community. This episode underlines the historical links in nuclear matters between the two countries, which go back to the dark days of 1940, in the aftermath of the French defeat, when Frédéric Joliot-Curie's team of Hans Halban and Lew Kowarski took refuge in London with their scientific work and the national stock of heavy water (D2O). The journey was made aboard the SS *Broompark*, a British cargo ship specially chartered for the mission. These events are part of the common history shared by the United Kingdom and France, who in recent times have always stuck together during difficult and dramatic moment.

In his book, Dautray confides:

I was not at all reluctant to contribute, even indirectly, to the construction of nuclear weapons. On the one hand, for me it was above all a question of solving mathematical, physical and technical problems. On the other hand, unlike many scientists at the CEA centre in Saclay, I had no doubt about the need to provide France with nuclear weapons. The radical pacifism of certain researchers of the Saclay Centre did not attract me … It simply seemed to me to be completely unrealistic: the few survivors of the death camps had not been liberated by non-violence. Nor had the non-violence of the millions of victims saved them.

4 August 1968: France goes thermonuclear

The risks associated with the power of a megaton test must be taken into account. The inhabitants of the Tureia atoll, located 100km away from Fagataufa, were evacuated to Papeete. Shelters for the local populations were set up on the islands of Gambier, Reao and Pukarua. A twin-engine Vautour IIB bomber from *Escadron de Marche 85 'Loire'* was ready for instant take-off to gather samples of air particles near the radioactive cloud expected during the test. Behind the technological challenge lay much politics and strategy. A thermonuclear warhead can produce much more power than an A-bomb, in a smaller size, while sparing plutonium, a scarce and expensive resource from uranium-based nuclear reactors. Since the UK had mastered the H-bomb, there was no question of France not also mastering this technology. Moreover, thermonuclear technology enhanced the military value of the ballistic missiles then being made in France.

Between the *pro domo* justifications of the CEA's military applications managers and the imperatives of secrecy, it is very difficult to establish a precise audit of an episode that now goes back more than half a century. The seal of secrecy will remain forever on the lively discussions that took place at the CEA centres of Bruyères le Châtel and Limeil-Brévane. In the aftermath of the Canopus test, French military nuclear ambitions were re-launched. The CEA's thermonuclear charges (the TN 60, then the TN61) were integrated during the 1970s into the warhead of ballistic missiles being prepared for submarines and the *Plateau d'Albion* nuclear base. By obtaining very high power in a small volume object, the '*Force de frappe*' could then undertake the development of different multiple warheads for its ballistic missiles, a step taken in 1985 with the M4 for submarines. At the same time, an H-weapon was installed in the front end of the ASMP (*Air-sol moyenne-portée*) supersonic missile carried on Mirage 2000N fighters and Mirage IV bombers from 1986 onwards.

At the same time, France was pushing forward its research on the neutron bomb, whose principle was also based on the phenomenon of fusion. Designated a 'reinforced radiation weapon', this lethal load would have been used in the Hadès mobile pre-strategic missiles, which were finally dismantled after 1996 at the end of the Cold War. In total, France conducted 210 nuclear tests (193 of which were made at the *Centre d'Expérimentations du Pacifique*), the last one on 27 January 1996 as part of a final campaign before the transition to full simulation.

2
CRITICAL TECHNOLOGIES

For the managers of the deterrence systems, the main objective was to master the key technologies necessary for the credibility of a platform, hence the success of the mission and national independence. The armament directorate (initially the DMA, then the DGA), and the CEA took up this mission in a direct relation with the armed forces and industry. The management of the project, from the state level to the design offices, always had in its scope a duality with civil applications. State-owned laboratories, tests centres and corporations worked under the coordination of the DGA. Nuclear energy, management of complex programmes, electronics, avionics and propulsion emerged as the critical domains for France to reach sovereignty. For example, the navigation unit of Concorde arose directly from military funding. In conventional weapons as well as the economy, these domains are the game changers and factors of credibility. Mastery of these domains eventually gave total control to Paris over its exports of defence products.

Top management: the mission of the DGA
The DGA, the French armament directorate, was – and remains – a powerful organization at the Ministry of Defence with full authority in contracting processes. The word 'Colbertism' describes its method of management, in reference to Jean-Baptiste Colbert, Prime Minister of Louis XIV, who developed the operational concept of direct intervention of the state in the economy through state-owned manufacture, infrastructure works and contacts with the private sector. Its top manager had the same hierarchic level as the chief of staff of the armed forces. The DGA covered all aspects of a programme, from specification to development, qualification and evaluation. Working with simulation tools, the DGA could define specifications. The following areas of expertise were developed in tests centres: hydrodynamics, hydro acoustics, aeronautical tests, weapons vulnerability, information security, integration of electronics, missiles and aircraft propulsion, flight tests, stealth techniques and protection against nuclear, biological and chemical aggressions. The DGA had some 20,000 engineers and technicians in 25 centres. In addition, these teams were involved in risk management and industrial policy, and supported the export of traditional weapons. At the final stage, the DGA delivered the technical specifications for military products. Reliability of 100 percent has always been mandatory. The DGA has organized working groups in the management of deterrence programmes, in particular 'Caelacante', the organization in charge of managing the design of nuclear submarines, their missiles and telecommunications. Effective partnerships have been forged with the CEA, CNES, the national space agency, CNRS (the National Scientific Research Centre) and ONERA, the aerospace national research organization.

A Benenice experimental missile and its re-entry vehicle. The *Office national d'Etudes et de Recherche Aerospatiale* was involved in the development of aircraft and ballistic missiles, in particular their aerodynamic design. (Onera Photo)

Eventually, the DGA became one of the main operational agencies of the nation in a global economy.

Nuclear energy and production of military plutonium: a voyage to Marcoule plant
Marcoule was the first French nuclear power plant. Its construction was decided by the five-year French nuclear plan launched in 1952 and implemented by Pierre Guillaumat, the managing director of the CEA. The plant secretly produced the plutonium for France's first atomic experiments. The plant is located in the Gard department, on the banks of the Rhône. Unlike the CEA units at that time (Fontenay-aux-Roses, Saclay, Grenoble), which focused on laboratory work, Marcoule was designed as an industrial complex. To hide its real purpose, nuclear power's military application was not mentioned at the launch of the project. In 1952, when the

The anechoic room at the electronic test centre at Bruz in Brittany, a facility of the DGA. In the centre is a Mirage III whose stealth features are being tested. (DGA Photo).

five-year nuclear plan was adopted, the decision to make the atomic bomb had not yet been taken, even if the nuclear plant provided the possibility of doing so. Backing for the project came from the silent support of political leaders such as Prime Minister René Pleven and Félix Gaillard, Secretary of State in charge of atomic affairs, who were instrumental in the origin of the 1952 programme. Marcoule houses three natural uranium reactors whose primary purpose is to produce plutonium, but also electricity for the economy. The first reactor, G1, is a cooled graphite fuel cell, whereas the other two (G2 and G3) are cooled by compressed gas. These reactors take the name of UNGG, for 'Natural Uranium Graphite Gas'. The first reactor was operational on 7 January 1956. On 28 October that year,

Zoe, the first French atomic reactor. (CEA Photo)

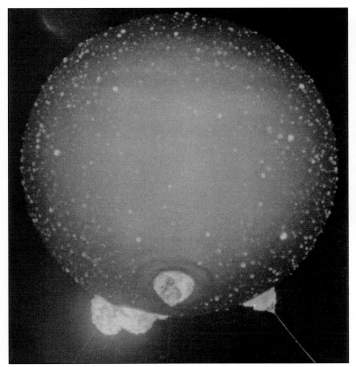

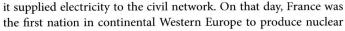

The fireball of the Procion thermonuclear test in the Pacific. French industry developed its own high-speed electronic devices. (CEA Photo)

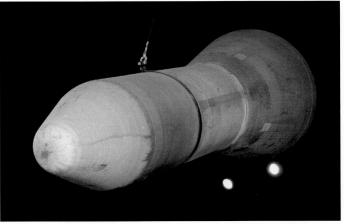

Prototype of a re-entry vehicle after a full-scale flight on display at the *Musée de l'air et de l'Espace*, Le Bourget. (Photo by author)

it supplied electricity to the civil network. On that day, France was the first nation in continental Western Europe to produce nuclear electricity. The complex also houses a fully automated plutonium extracting plant and a graphite production facility. In the days following his arrival at the Elysée Palace, the then Prime Minister de Gaulle visited the facility on 2 August 1958.

Command, control, communication, hardening and computing

From his bunker, a concrete structure under the Élysée Palace, the President of France can transmit orders to the nuclear units. From his Louis XV-style office, he can walk to the Jupiter Command Post, a shelter equipped with communication systems to enable

Ignition of the propulsion stage of a ballistic missile at the Saint Médard test centre in the Bordeaux area. A strong effort was achieved in the solid propulsion domain. (Photo Aerospatiale, now Ariangroup)

Hypersonic aerodynamic tunnel used to test re-entry vehicles, a key test instrument of the LRBA, the *Laboratoire de Recherche Balistic et Aérodynamic*. (LRBA Photo).

A prototype of an inertial navigation unit designed at the beginning of the 1960s by the Sagem company. Works was carried out on size and weight features of the unit, in compliance with the precision of the navigation. (Photo Safran Electronics & Defence/Sagem; now Safran)

Dassault Electronique and SAT (future subsidiary of Sagem). At the beginning of the 1960s, dedicated teams were set up within the aerospace industries to integrate calculators and data processing. Bull, a state-owned company, set up within the 'Calcul' plan a programme to produce the computers for the bomb. As a tribute to the quality of this French sector, in 1984 the Pentagon chose the RITA system of Thomson-CSF to create a tactical radio network for the US Army. The programme was renamed as Mobile Subscriber Equipment. Satellite communication was decided upon in January 1980. Named Syracuse (*Système de radiocommunication utilisant un satellite*), this project had to ensure a robust military link between mainland France and overseas forces, notably combat ships. The first generation of these geostationary satellites was launched in 1984 from a European Ariane booster.

Two French Air Force bases ensure operational links: Taverny (in a northern suburb of Paris) and Lyon Mont-Verdun (north of Lyon). The fleet of C-160H Astarte aircraft was among the most spectacular programmes of the period. The four aircraft were delivered to the air force between 1981 and 1987. The Astarte is the equivalent of the US Navy's E-6 Mercury Tacamo ('Take charge and move out'). The aircraft is equipped with a Rockwell VLF transmitter, its integration resulting from a cooperation with Thomson-CSF. The system includes trailed wire antennae. The *Armée de l'Air* retired its Astartes in 2002.

Inertial navigation: a demanding discipline

The challenge of inertial navigation dates back to the earliest times, when man decided to venture out to sea, then in the air and ultimately in space. As he moved away from the coast, he had no other point of reference than the sun during the day, the stars by clear night. The compass, astrolabe, sextant and clocks (for time reference) came to assist in distant explorations. From 1945, the imperative of precision imposed itself on atomic platforms. A navigation unit was created using a set of inertial sensors: three gyroscopes and three accelerometers. Working with a computer, it provided heading and position in the absence of external radio sources. Everything would be perfect so long as the equipment's accuracy did not gradually deteriorate during the trip, any deviation affecting accuracy against the target. Deviation would be further amplified by the combination of speed and distance. It was therefore necessary to recalibrate the instrument with known external references: stars, geographic points and radio signals from ground beacons or satellites.

Inertial navigation is a pillar of sovereignty in the sense that its mastery gives the nation full control of its weapons without depending on anyone else. Tests of the first Sagem inertial unit were carried out on a twin-engine Nord 2501 aircraft at the flight test centre of Brétigny in 1961. Work was applied to compactness and performance. In 1965, the E27 system had reached a size equivalent

the president and his advisers to manage the worst scenario and be in direct contact at all times with other foreign leaders or military command posts. Initially, the bunker was built for President Albert Lebrun in 1940 for protection against German bombs. The decision to reuse the facility as a command post was made by President Valéry Giscard d'Estaing. It has been operational since 1978. Servicing the president, a global C4ISR system of systems had been deployed on specifications written by the DGA and the armed forces. In 1956, Maurice Ponte was director of electronics specialists Thomson-CSF in charge of technologies. Aware of the ambitions of the nation, the future CEO of the group decided to express his view in *Revue Défense Nationale*, where he claimed a critical role for electronics in nuclear forces. Electronics was a new expertise financed by long-term and costly programmes awarded to Aerospatiale, Alcatel, Thomson-CSF,

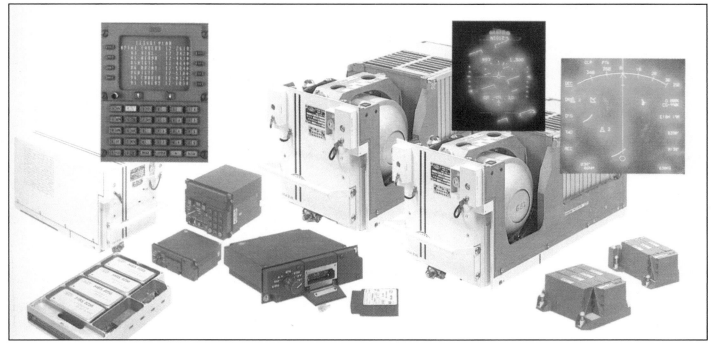

Etna navigation systems of the Super Étendard. (Sagem/Safran)

The Navigation unit of a ballistic missile. This device is on display at the *Musée de l'air et de l'Espace* at Le Bourget. (Photo by author)

also applied to Concorde, the supersonic aircraft receiving a Sagem inertial navigation system. Licenses were in addition acquired from the American manufacturer Kerfot. To this end, US government authorization was required. For the Redoutable-class SSBNs, the LRBA and Sagem developed the CIN M2B platform. At the end of the 1970s, a third generation of inertial systems appeared for the new M4 ballistic missile that featured multiple warheads. The experimental *Gymnote* submarine took part in development tests. For the Super Étendard planned for 1978, Sagem designed Etna, which was connected to the vessel's alignment system. The engineers also worked on Pluton, Hadès and the Uliss52 mechanical inertial unit for the Mirage 2000. From the 1980s onwards, mechanical sensors were followed by laser gyro sensors, technology installed on the Rafale fighter jets. In parallel, electronics for missiles became a new expertise at Dassault Electronique for the MD.620 Jericho, the ballistic missile developed for Israel. Indeed, the avionics developed for the Jerico are re-used for the Pluton missile.

to that of a shoebox, and contributed to the successful launch of the Asterix satellite by the Diamant launcher. This sector was mobilized from the 1960s with some very heavy investment. Missile design experts LRBA (the Ballistic and Aerodynamic Research Laboratory in Vernon, northern France) mobilized its teams, Sagem being entrusted for the industrialization of the solutions for the strategic vectors. The domain was managed by two sectors of the DGA: the *Service Technique Aéronautique* (aviation) and the *Service Technique des Engins* (missiles). Sagem's know-how also benefitted from civil activities, the company having been selected to ensure the maintenance of the inertial platforms installed on the fleet of Air France Boeing 707s from 1967. The duality with the civil world

Electronic warfare and avionics: emergence of new disciplines

French industry was a pioneer in the emerging domain of electronic warfare. The Eiffel Tower is not only an iconic building attracting tourists, but also an intelligence system. It is the reason why this elegant metal construction was saved in 1914 by General Gustave

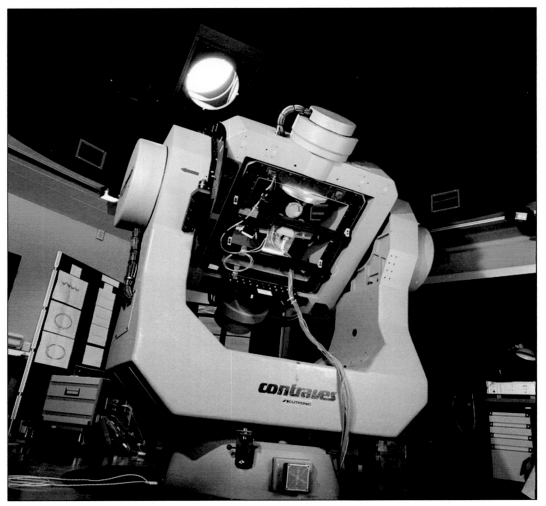

A three-axis table, a device of the *Laboratoire de Recherche Balistic et Aérodynamic*. (LRBA Photo)

Ferrié, chief of the signal corps, who demonstrated the capability of the Eiffel Tower to listen to German radio-communications. In the Cold War, boosted by the lessons of the wars in Vietnam and the Middle East, French programmes covered all domains of electronic warfare (EW): intelligence, electronic support, electronic attack, escort jamming and self-protection. Marcel Dassault, in a pioneer strategy, had pointed out the importance of an alliance between fighter aircraft and combat electronics, hence the creation of Dassault Electronique. Its arrival in the industrial landscape paralleled the ambitions of Thomson-CSF. In addition, Matra and Aerospatiale specialized in missiles. The Mirage IV was the first vector to receive a comprehensive self-protection suite: two jammers inside the fuselage, dubbed Agacette and Agasol, plus decoy dispensers. Under the delta wing, a podded jammer and a decoy-launcher could be loaded. In the domain

The *Henri Poincaré*, the telemetry vessel of the French Navy used for development and testing of missiles. To prepare its own nuclear force, French industry was involved in the development of test systems. (Marine Nationale)

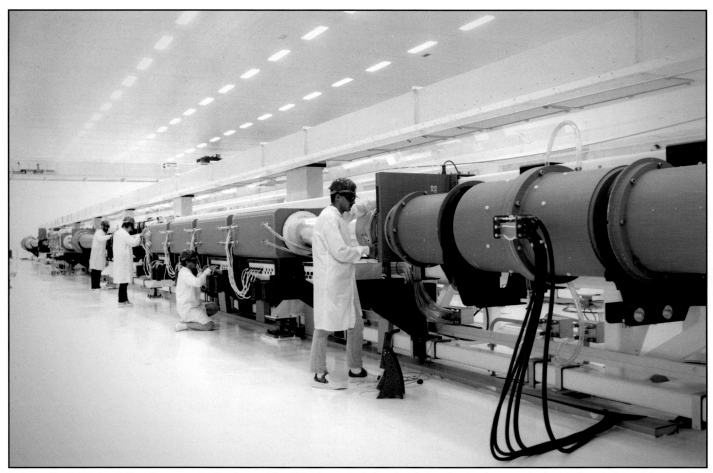

Delivered in 1985, the Phébus laser was the first laser of the CEA. The commission decided to develop its expertise in this domain in anticipation of the transition to the nuclear simulation programmes. (CEA Photo)

A C.160 Transall NG Astarte relay aircraft under the antennas of an electronic laboratory at Gramat in order to evaluate its hardening features against high-power electronic pulses. (DGA Photo)

Taverny air base, the command post of the French strategic forces. The strategic C3s were all made in France. Scientific knowhow was encouraged in selective engineering high schools such as the *École Normale Supérieure*, *École Supérieure d'Electricité* and Sup Telecom. Officers of the Signal Corps were tasked to follow the entire course, like any student. (*Forces Aériennes Stratégiques*)

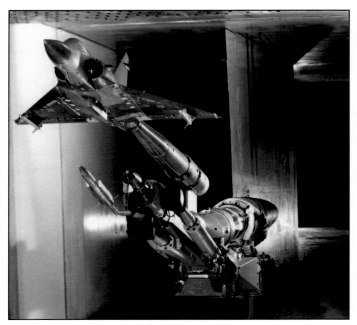

Mock-up of a Mirage 2000 and its ASMP missile in a wind tunnel of Onera, the national aerospace research agency, to develop the separation sequence. (Onera Photo)

of suppression of enemy air defences, the air force combined jammers and AS-37 Martel missiles. This solution was integrated on the Mirage IIIE and Jaguar. The year 1976 was a milestone, with the Jaguars of the 2/11 Vosges squadron receiving BOA escort jamming pods, the defence systems receiving solutions to reduce detection. Protection and integrity relied on cyphering techniques and frequency hopping. In Brittany, near Rennes, the CELAr (*Centre d'Electronique de l'Armement*), an expertise centre of the DGA, came to the forefront by building an anechoic chamber to develop stealth

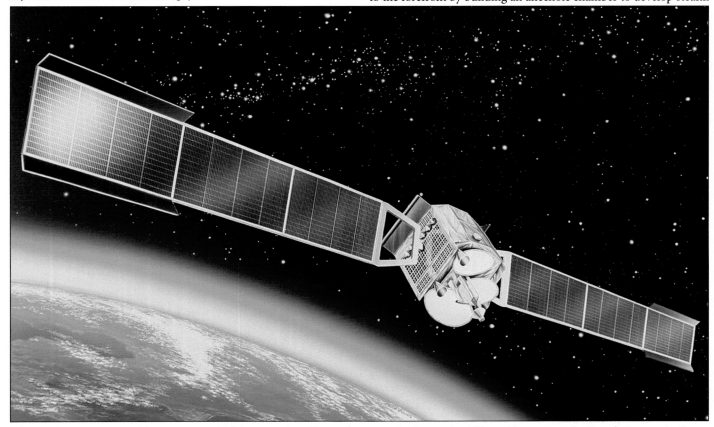

Telecom IA was a commercial programme which integrated a military telecommunication payload. Named Syracuse, or *Système de Communication utilisant un satellite*, the first generation of space assets of the French MoD were put into a geostationary orbit by an Ariane 3 launcher on 4 August 1984, 8 August 1985 and 11 March 1988. (Airbus)

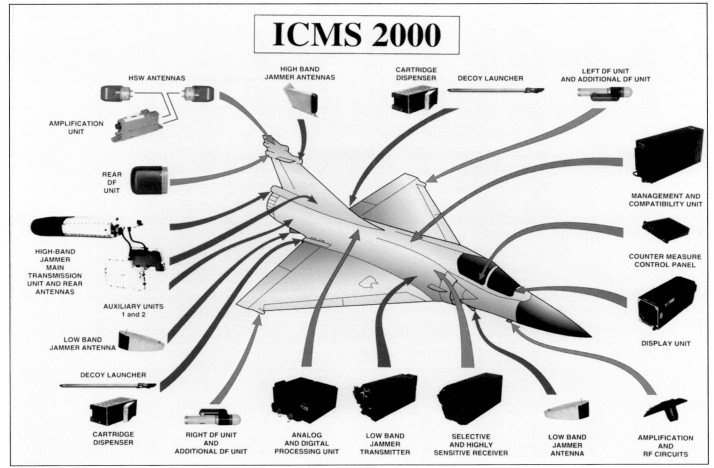

The Mirage 2000 was the first combat aircraft to receive a comprehensive integrated self-protection system, which was developed by Thomson-CSF for the electronic sub-systems (sensors, jammers), in cooperation with Matra (decoy-launchers) and Lacroix (chaffs and flares). The solution was applied to all sub-variants of the Mirage 2000, conventional or nuclear. (Thomson-CSF; now Thales)

architectures. The solutions were applied on cruise missiles, and in a final stage on the Rafale. Anti-submarine sonars are also part of this domain, contributing to the protection of the oceanic strike force.

Aircraft and missiles: the mastery of high performance propulsion

Established on 9 August 1946, in the vicinity of the capital, the CEPr (Aero-engine test centre) was focused on testing engines of missiles or aircraft in simulated flight conditions. Before the Second World War, the CEPr was known as the *Centre d'essais des moteurs et des hélices*. Based on the *Plateau de Saclay*, CEPr worked on new propulsion techniques. Its facilities offered extreme conditions: very low or high temperatures, high altitude, icing and high Mach numbers. Its wind tunnels could simulate flight at high altitude – more than Mach 4 – and control its aerodynamic evolutions in extreme conditions. The CEPr was at the crossroads of the design departments of Sereb and Snecma and worked under the management of the DGA Tests division on every aviation programme: Ouragan, Vautour, Super Mystère, Fouga Magister, Noratlas, Caravelle

Mock-up of the aerodynamic tunnel to test a ramjet supersonic missile in a simulated high-altitude environment. The mock-up was displayed at the Paris Air Show in 1999. (Photo by author)

and helicopters. Between 1965 and 1970, its teams were tasked with heavy propulsion systems in preparation for the first generation of strategic missiles. Its assets included a dedicated silo to study the launch sequence. An additional facility simulated the ignition of a booster over an altitude of 90,000ft. The first test of such design was achieved in July 1965. A CEPr annex building was built at Saint-Médard-en-Jalles in the vicinity of Bordeaux to test heavy boosters. Proving its expertise, the CEPr worked on the Olympus 593B engine of Concorde and the Atar 9K of Mirage IV, the M53 of the Mirage 2000, then the M88 for the Rafale and in the 1970s and 1980s the ASMP missile. The CEPr is now named *DGA Essais Propulseurs*.

3
MIRAGE IV: MORE THAN A STRATEGIC MILITARY OBJECT

During the 1960s, the first decade of French deterrence, the Mirage IV was the only asset to deliver the bomb. In its communications, the Strategic Air Forces Command always liked to humorously mention this legacy to be 'the first nuclear component' in a friendly rivalry with the French Navy. This is true from an historic point of view. From an aeronautic point of view, the Mirage IV embodied an aeronautic French pride. This status is shared with Concorde, which is British for the British but French for the French.

A formation of Mirage IVAs in the wake of a C-135FR Stratotanker, both components of the Strategic Air Force Command. Two routes of penetration to their targets through Soviet air defences were planned: one to the north and a second after transit of the Mediterranean Sea. (*Forces Aériennes Stratégiques*)

The Mirage IV featured amazing performance. It was the structural pillar of a new command, the *Commandement des Forces Aériennes Stratégiques*, or Strategic Air Forces Command. COFAS has been created by a decree of President Charles de Gaulle on 14 January 1964. The image of the wide delta wing is almost always associated with the C-135 Stratotanker, which was purchased in the US. On the day of its first use in October 1964, the Mirage IV was the only European military aircraft able to maintain a speed of Mach 2 for over 30 minutes. The Dassault creation had an incredible operational longevity, lasting 42 years. Its elegant silhouette survived all its rivals, in particular the B-58 Hustler, which retired in January 1970, just a decade after its entry within the Strategic Air Forces Command. It also survived the British TSR-2, an ambitious project

In addition to its politico-military mission, the Mirage IV was a record-breaking aircraft. On 19 September 1960, René Bigand climbed into the fuselage of the Mirage IV 01. Taking off from Melun-Villaroche, he broke the world closed-circuit speed record at an average speed of 1,822km/h. The aircraft maintained Mach 1.9 for 33 minutes. The speed record was taken several months later on 14 January 1961 by a B-58 Hustler at an average speed of 2,067km/h. (Dassault Aviation)

A Mirage IV before a fight test. On 1 December 1959, a Mirage IV reached an altitude of 18,000m and achieved Mach 2. In June 1959, the aircraft flew over the Paris Air Show at Le Bourget. The aircraft had a length of 23.5m, a wingspan of 11.85m and a maximum take-off weight of 32 tons. (Dassault Aviation).

The front cover of *Interavia* international aviation magazine published in 1963. You can clearly see the atom bomb under the fuselage of a Mirage IV. In the early years of the Cold War, information heralding the reality of the atomic strike force was seen as mandatory. (Interavia)

cancelled in 1965. Among other friendly competitors were the Avro CF-105 Arrow, an ambitious Canadian interceptor cancelled in 1959. The five last Mirage IVs remained in operation until 2005 in a reconnaissance configuration, thus enjoying a longer career than the SR-71 Blackbird and even Concorde. In terms of military culture, for the French armed forces, the Mirage IV was a flying academy in overseas operations. For many aviation observers, the Mirage IV was a legend, the expression of French wings. In a symposium held in September 1984 on the nuclear history of France, General Maurin, first commanding officer of COFAS, gave it a glowing testimony, mentioning a meeting with journalists invited to visit a nuclear base in the mid-1960s to see the aircraft and meet the crews on alert. Answering a journalist, one pilot answered: "I am not afraid of my responsibility, because our force is a retaliation force, therefore, I will have no hesitation to launch a bomb on a country which had decided to attack us."

Design and development: a specific management

The diplomatic lessons of the Suez adventure prompted the political leaders of France to set up a strategic force. The final specifications jointly defined by government authorities and Dassault were approved on 20 March 1957. Coming back into office in June 1958, General de Gaulle gave the idea a boost. The scheme was to rapidly produce a strategic bomber, then a ballistic force later. The execution of work in the project was impressive considering the technological challenges. In May 1956, Guy Mollet's administration drew up a specification for a refuellable supersonic bomber capable of carrying a 3-ton payload a distance of 2,000km (without aerial refuelling). The aircraft was not officially launched by Charles de Gaulle's

An advertisement for Dassault Aviation in the 1960s. Its message read: "The Mirage is as invulnerable to enemy blows as the Mirage is elusive to the desert traveller." Marcel Dassault himself explained the name choices for his aircraft: "It was in memory of a much-loved book of my childhood, *Le Docteur Mystère*, that I called my first supersonic airplane the Mystère. My Mirage airplanes, because of their attack and evasion capacities, are as invulnerable to enemy fire as a mirage is unreachable for a desert traveller, hence the name Mirage." (Dassault Aviation)

The assembly line of the Mirage IV at Merignac Airport. Between 1960 and 1966, 62 aircraft were produced exclusively for the French armed forces, even though South Africa and Israel were both interested in the aircraft to build up their own strategic force, as was Australia. In the end, Pretoria obtained clearance for the purchase of Mirage IIIs and British Blackburn Buccaneers. (Author's collection)

Maintenance being carried out on an Atar 9K engine. This version integrated an improved combustion chamber and turbine blade cooling reducing consumption. The engine could give a maximum thrust of 6,700kg. Like all the Dassault combat aircraft, the Mirage IV was designed to be easy to maintain in operational zones. (Snecma; now Safran)

several successes in the civil and military sectors: the Caravelle liner (maiden flight on 27 May 1955), Mystere IV (28 September 1952), Mirage III combat aircraft (17 November 1956) and Vautour (16 October 1960). These French-made aircraft were combat-proven in the hands of Israeli pilots during the Suez War in 1956. The prototype was ordered by the Ministry of Defence on 28 November 1956 without any mention of a nuclear mission. The milestones were rapidly taken. A special organization was initiated between the authorities and industry to develop the aircraft as quickly as possible. Decisions were taken through letters from the minister sent to the main contractor. Contracts were then confirmed, thereby avoiding heavy procedures that would have slowed down the work. As a result, the Mirage IV was

administration, but by Mollet, a leader of the socialist party during the *IVe Republique*. A design by Dassault was selected. A decade after 1945, the aeronautic industry had been restored and recorded developed ahead of schedule and on a lower budget than forecast: a unique case in the history of armaments, and not only in France.

A crew on alert gets on board the bomber for a training mission. Just seconds before, the two officers were in an alert room waiting for an order to arrive. (*Forces Aériennes Stratégiques*)

World records

On 17 June 1959, Roland Glavany, a test pilot for Dassault, took off in a Mirage IV for the first time at 10:20 a.m. from Melun-Villaroche Airport, 50km south of Paris. The flight lasted 40 minutes. For its third flight, on 20 June, the first prototype was cleared to make a pass over the Paris Air Show at Le Bourget, President de Gaulle being among the public in attendance. On 30 June 1960, the administration ordered 50 aircraft, the first five being delivered in 1963. Between 1964 and 1966, all 50 Mirage IVs were delivered. On 4 November 1965, a new contract sealed the acquisition of 12 additional aircraft. The last aircraft was delivered in March 1968. A total of 66 aircraft were built in a project that had involved 300 companies. In addition, the programme consolidated for the following decades the relationship between the DGA at the state level, Dassault and its sub-contractors, notably Thomson-CSF for the electronics systems and Snecma for the engines, among many others. Four prototypes were produced for development. The first, 01, left the factory at the beginning of 1959 but suffered an accident on 13 February 1959. Aircraft 02, completed on 12 October 1961, was used for bombing tests. The 03 achieved its first flight on 1 June 1962 and was used for testing the navigation system and the first in-flight refuelling manoeuvres. The fourth aircraft, equipped with Snecma Atar 9 engines, began its tests on 23 January 1963 in Melun-Villaroche. With regard to its avionics and engine, this aircraft corresponded to the series production aircraft. For the domestic aviation industry, "the Mirage IV is the first truly integrated weapon system in France", according to Luc Berger, official historian of Dassault Aviation.

The aircraft and the bomb

The Mirage IV shared design features and an external resemblance to the Mirage III, featuring a tailless delta wing and a single vertical fin. However, the wing was significantly thinner to allow supersonic performance and had a thickness-chord ratio of 3.8 percent at the root and 3.2 percent at the tip. This wing was the thinnest built in Europe at the time and one of the thinnest in the world.

The Mirage IVA had a fuselage recess under the engines which could hold a single nuclear weapon, the AN-11 (40kt) initially and then the AN-22 (60kt). To improve take-off performance and range, the Mirage IV could have 12 Jato solid-fuel rockets diagonally below the wing flaps. A self-protection electronic warfare system arrived just in time for the first deployment in the 1960s. This suite was composed of Agacette and Agassol jammers. For secret missions, these electronics would help the plane cross Soviet air defences (in particular the network of SA2 and SA6 surface-to-air missiles). The aircraft claimed the world speed record when, at 5:05 p.m. on 19 September 1960, René Bigand took off

In its concrete hangar, a Mirage IVA is fully operational ready for take-off, the AN-22 bomb being already loaded. (*Forces Aériennes Stratégiques*)

One of the 12 Boeing C-135FR Stratotankers purchased in 1962. In 2022, part of the fleet was still always in the flight lines of the French Air Force. (*Forces Aériennes Stratégiques*)

A Mirage III of the CIFAS 328 training squadron. (*Forces Aériennes Stratégiques*)

from Melun-Villaroche in the Mirage IV 01 and achieved 1,822km/h over a 1,000km closed circuit. On 23 September, the aircraft pushed the record to 1,972km/h on a 500km closed circuit, flying between Mach 2.08 and Mach 2.14. As a nuclear weapon system, the aircraft had to be validated with its strategic payload. This was done during Operation *Tamouré* on 19 July 1966, when the Mirage IV 09 provided by the Gascogne squadron fired a live AN-11 nuclear weapon off Mururoa atoll.

Mirage IVP and ASMP missile

The Mirage IVP was an upgrade programme using the original fleet of Mirage IVAs to take account of new and improved air defences.

Missions now had to be achieved at low altitude and high speed, with self-protection improved and the weapon released at a stand-off distance from the target. The programme picked out 18 aircraft to receive the upgrades. Work was prioritized on the integration of the ASMP missile. Two others areas were part of the upgrade programme: electronic warfare self-protection and work on the airframe to augment its service life. Developed by Thomson-CSF, the EW part of the upgrade comprised a Serval radar-warning receiver, Barracuda jamming pods combined with two decoy launchers, a Boz dispenser and another decoy-launcher integrated under the aft section of the fuselage. The ASMP was a stand-off missile, a new credibility. Development of the missile was initiated in March 1978

This Falcon 20 business jet was specially modified to train the crews of the Mirage IV, the aircraft integrating an exact reproduction of the bomber's cockpit in the cabin. (Photo by Gilles Rolle/*Armée de l'Air*

The C-135FR and Mirage IV, the operational combination of the FAS. A special beacon on the tanker allowed the Mirage IV to continue its route. The two aircraft produced a new culture in the French Air Force focused on long-distance missions and operations from an overseas base, a new know-how that would be transferred to tactical aviation forces. (Dassault Aviation)

in order to replace the free-fall bombs, the AN.22 of the Mirage IV and the AN.52 of the Jaguar, Mirage IIIE and Super Étendard. The programme was entrusted to Aerospatiale as main contractor, under the supervision of DGA. It featured an innovative ramjet propulsion system, whose development had been decided upon in 1972. Onera, the *Office national d'études et de recherches aéronautique* (National Research Laboratory of Aeronautics), was part of the R&D sequence; tests in its wind tunnel in Modane (Savoy) demonstrated that a wing fixed on the fuselage was useless, a conclusion that improved the aircraft's stealth performances. Propulsion of the missile worked in

two phases: first, a solid-propellant booster was ignited just after separation until a speed of Mach 2; then this section was ejected and the ramjet was ignited, giving a speed of over Mach 3. Considering its low radar cross-section, the missile could not be intercepted. During mission preparation in the squadron, parameters of the flight path and the mode of attack were loaded in the navigation system. The new nuclear warhead, a TN81 in the official nomenclature, was designed and produced by the CEA. Sub-contractors worked on 20 percent of the project: the central computer was designed by Dassault Electronic and the navigation system by Sagem.

In place of the atomic weapon, the Mirage IV could accommodate a CT-52 photo-reconnaissance pod. In this configuration, the Mirage IV was deployed for long-range missions in support of national defence objectives or reinforcing the intelligence data, notably on the new combat ships of the Soviet Union. (Photo by author)

A Jato take-off of a prototype of the Mirage IVP, equipped with an ASMP missile, a vision of the update of the French strategic force in the 1980s. (Dassault Aviation)

Aerospatiale conducted 1,300 simulated flights on a test bench at its Bourges factory and in the Palaiseau facility of Onera. The first live test was achieved on 23 June 1983, then on 5 March 1985, the engineers at the Landes test centre conducted the first flight from a Mirage 2000N. On 10 December 1985, an ASMP was launched by a Mirage IV and exceeded Mach 3 over 150 miles. Thirteen qualification flights were achieved between 1986 and 1989, the last ones with the French Navy, in addition to flights from a launch pad. According to public sources, 87 ASMPs were delivered to the armed forces, the last 11 in 1991. The missile was officially in service after a *synthèse* flight conducted on 19 March 1986 with a Mirage IV. Along with special bunkers at air bases, the missile could be kept on board the aircraft carriers *Clemenceau* and *Foch*, the modification being achieved in 1989. The payload was a thermonuclear warhead able to produce 150kt. Capable of tactical anti-force or strategic strikes, the ASMP allowed the fusion of tactical forces and a strategic unit on one unique nuclear bomber, aiming for a global deterrence mission entrusted to the coming fleet of Mirage 2000Ns planned for the 1990s.

Strategic reconnaissance

The recce version of the Mirage IV was a success and came into operational status. The system relied on a CT-52, or Container Technique, an intelligence imagery pod which integrated a comprehensive ensemble of cameras. The strategic reconnaissance mission was tasked to the CIFAS, the Instruction Centre of the Strategic Air Forces. Based in Bordeaux Airport, this discreet unit conducted long-range photographic missions involving the last 12 Mirage IVs of the series equipped with the optic pod. The system had mechanical features in the bay of the AN-22 atomic bomb. The CT-52 integrated three Omera 36 HA cameras and a Wild RC 8F, from which pictures could be taken between 150 and 56,000ft. Testing was run between 1969 and 1971. One of the missions was to photograph Soviet warships. Under the command of Cofas, these missions were carried out in close collaboration with the French Navy. Receiving the support of C-135FR refuelling tankers, the Mirage IVs searched, often in the Mediterranean Sea, for the new Soviet Kiev-class aircraft carriers, Moskova helicopter carriers and even the latest generations of missile destroyers (in particular Kashin and Krivak-class units). A typical task of the Cold War, these operations, with the aircraft kept on alert, also targeted Soviet submarines on the surface. Shared with France's allies, the information gathered underlined the attachment of the French armed forces to the defence of the Atlantic Alliance. Mirage IVs and Stratotankers built a new air force operational culture focused on overseas operations, notably in Africa. The aircraft conducted missions over Chad in the 1970s and 1980s during operations intended to stop the territorial ambitions of Libyan dictator Colonel Gaddafi. Their main mission was to prepare raids by Mirage IVs in Central Europe in cooperation with signal intelligence assets. The Mirage IV was also an interesting tool to improve the training of the allies against the Tu-22 Blinder and Backfire, their Soviet equivalents. In the Mediterranean, playing the aggressors, Mirage IVs regularly simulated raids against US aircraft carriers in order to improve the training of their F-14 Tomcat crews against supersonic targets. For that purpose, the Mirages were equipped with the CT-52 photographic pod. Pictures were taken vertically over the ship as evidence of its 'neutralization'. The crews were then invited aboard the US ships for debriefings, friendly chats over coffee and an exclusive tour of the vessel.

The success of the Mirage IV led to studies for several versions which never went beyond the project stage. In this domain, the

The place of the Mirage IV in the strategic deterrence stance was reduced due to the permanence at sea of nuclear submarines in the second part of the 1970s. However, at the end of the 1980s, 15 Mirage IV were maintained and upgraded to integrate the new ASMP missile, a programme intended to maintain its credibility. In this picture, we can identify the two electronic warfare self-protection pods (outside underwing drop tanks) in addition to a single ASMP nuclear missile under the centreline. (Photo *Armée de l'Air*)

Dassault design bureau proposed the Mirage IVB, an enlarged version of the original aircraft. Design drawings gave the aircraft a length of 27.8m and a maximum take-off weight of 56 tons. Without in-flight refuelling, the plane would have been able to fly more than 4,400km. Engineers had also imagined a Mirage IVE, a configuration dedicated to electronic warfare for intelligence or escort jamming in support of distant raids over enemy territory. However, this version also was cancelled in favor of a strategic Sigint aircraft, the four-engined DC-8 Sarigue. A naval version in a single-seat configuration was also proposed by Dassault to equip the Verdun class, a new design of large aircraft carrier. This idea was abandoned at the beginning of the 1970s for economic reasons, but also because it was seen as a weak operational concept regarding 'sufficient deterrence'.

Carrying exclusively the CT-52 pod after 1996, the remaining Mirage IVs of the 1/91 Gascogne squadron found a new legitimacy after the fall of the Berlin Wall, the recce configuration aircraft playing a crucial role in all the international crises and conflicts of the post-Cold War era until their withdrawal from service in 2005.

OPERATION TAMOURÉ, A WORLD TOUR AND A LIVE ATOMIC TEST

Operation *Tamouré* began in May 1966 with a long flight from mainland France to French Polynesia. The name of the mission was inspired by a Polynesian folk dance. The decision to conduct a full-scale nuclear test at the Pacific test centre was made on 30 October 1964 at a defence council formally presided over by Charles de Gaulle at the Elysée Palace. The green light was given at BA 118 (Air Base 118) at Mont-de-Marsan in south-western France). It was a complex mission, tasking two Mirage IVs of the EB-1/91 Gascogne 39 squadron and three C-135F tankers. The group's task was to carry out a live test of a 60kt AN-21 at the Pacific Experimentation Centre. Parts of the atomic object were transported by a Douglas DC-8 of the GLAM squadron (*Groupement de liaisons ministérielles*). At 9:00 a.m. on 10 May, a Mirage IV took off for the first transatlantic voyage achieved by a French combat aircraft, heading to Otis Air Force Base in Falmouth, Massachusetts. Unfortunately, upon arriving in French Polynesia, the Mirage IV was damaged when landing, hitting an excavator on the 3,380m runway of BA 185 in Hao. It had to return to France by sea, immediately being replaced by Mirage IV 09. After being postponed four times due to adverse weather, meteorological conditions were deemed favourable on 18 July and the Mirage IV was put on alert the following day at 4:00 a.m. local time. At 05:05 a.m., the aircraft dropped its AN-11 atomic bomb off the coast of Mururoa. A USAF Stratotanker and the USS *Richfield* were in the vicinity an hour after. As soon as the atomic cloud was formed, some of the Vautours of the 85 Loire

squadron took samples of the fallout. For this mission, these 10 aircraft used special air-to-air missiles or, more dangerously, traversed the atomic mushroom cloud. On 25 July, the FAS detachment in Polynesia took off from Hao for the return trip to Europe, following the same route in reverse. The Mirage IV and C-135 landed at night at Mont-de-Marsan on 28 July; Operation *Tamouré* was over. The Mirage IV would never again be tasked to carry out real atomic tests. They were no longer necessary, as the trio of Mirage IV, AN bomb and Stratotanker had demonstrated their operational credibility.

Just before take-off for Operation *Tamouré*: in the cockpit, Commandant Dubroca. The navigator, Captain Caubert, is visible on a ladder to the rear cockpit. (*Forces Aériennes Stratégiques*)

Load operation of an AN-21 bomb in preparation for the *Tamouré* operation. (*Forces Aériennes Stratégiques*)

A Mirage IVA in full afterburner mode on the runway of Hao atoll. Note the AN-21 under the fuselage, which yielded 50 kilotons. The aircraft returned safely to base. (*Forces Aériennes Stratégiques*)

THE MIRAGE IVA IN THE STRATEGIC AIR FORCE

At the highest level of deployment, the Mirage IVA equipped the following squadrons:

EB-1/91 Gascogne, founded on 1 October 1964	BA 118, Mont-de-Marsan;
EB-2/94 Marne, 24 February 1965	BA 113, Saint-Dizier;
EB-2/91 Bretagne, 1 April 1965	BA 120, Cazaux;
EB-3/91 Beauvaisis, 1 June 1965	BA 110, Creil;
EB-3/93 Sambre, 6 July 1965	BA 103, Cambrai;
EB-2/93 Cévennes, 31 July 1965 (30)	BA 115, Orange;
EB-1/93 Guyenne, 15 October 1965	BA 125, Istres;
EB-1/94 Bourbonnais, 1 March 1966	BA 702, Avord;
EB-3/94 Arbois, 1 June 1966	BA 116, Luxeuil;
CIFAS 328, 25 May 1964	BA 106, Bordeaux.

(*Centre d'instruction des Forces aériennes stratégiques*)

The 12 Boeing C-135F Stratotankers (including three aircraft on alert) were deployed in three squadrons (ERV, *Escadrons de ravitaillement en vol*): ERV-4/91 Landes, 1 January 1964, at BA 118, Mont-de-Marsan; ERV-4/93 Aunis, 13 July 1965, 32 at BA 125, Istres; and ERV-4/94 Sologne, 15 April 1966, BA 702, Avord.

4
BALLISTIC MISSILES OF THE STRATEGIC TRIAD

In 1967, General Charles Ailleret, the French chief of staff, published an article in *Revue Defense Nationale* In which he wrote: "If France wants to be able to avoid the risks that could threaten it, the Nation must have a significant quantity of long-range ballistic weapons, the action of which could deter those who would decide, from any place in the world, to destroy us." President de Gaulle had validated the text.

This sums up the motivation of the strategic triad. Following the first operational Mirage IV squadron in October 1964, the ambition was continuing, with a target to deploy rapidly the comprehensive nuclear force General de Gaulle wanted to have. Designed on the American model, the triad had to be operational in 1970. Engineers had to invent everything, exploring domains they have never been before: nuclear propulsion, ballistic missiles, space, operations in harsh environments. In order to speed up the development, and considering the costs, special tests facilities were set up to validate the potential solutions. Regarding ballistic missiles, these efforts were open to a commercial space programme that would eventually provide the Ariane family of launchers. The use of these ballistic armaments was part of the concept of a massive retaliation strike against demographic targets. Two milestones were achieved at the beginning of the 1970s: on 2 August 1971, nine S-2 missiles were ready to be used in the silos of *Plateau d'Albion*; six months later, in February 1972, the nuclear submarine *Le Redoutable* left its l'Ile Longue base for its first deterrence patrol.

Plateau d'Albion: a missile base in the Alps of Haute-Provence

The concept of SSBS (*Sol-Sol Balistique Stratégique*) weapons in the mountains of southern Provence was directly inspired by the US Air Force model. Officially, the base is named Saint-Christol, but for the French people, the facilities, missiles and their reinforced concreted shelters are popularized under the name of *Plateau d'Albion*. The origin of the missile base goes back to 2 May 1963, when the Defence Council endorsed the creation of a force of 20–30 IRBMs (Intermediate-Range Ballistic Missiles). The base covers an area of 800km² that is divided into 27 individual locations, all connected by a road network. In May 1965, instructions were received to install the ground-to-ground missile force on *Plateau d'Albion*. Other locations for the force had rapidly been dismissed: Corsica, the Massif Central and the Vosges mountains (the latter option in particular due to its position close to France's eastern border). To

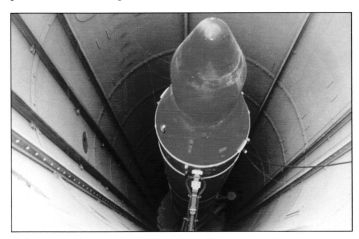

In its launch-silo is an S-2, the first generation of ground-to-ground ballistic missiles. The S-2 was a medium range vector with a single re-entry vehicle. Its purpose was to be an anti-demographic weapon, in line with the mutual assured destruction concept written into the deterrence strategy. (*Forces Aériennes Stratégiques*)

One of the 18 S-3D missiles ready for launch. With a range of 3,500km, they coud be used as a retaliatory strike at very short notice (minutes) upon the order of the President of the Republic. The S-3D featured better capability in term of penetration performances and a thermonuclear payload of 1 megaton. (*Forces Aériennes Stratégiques*)

An aerial view of *Plateau d'Albion*, the missile base of the Strategic Air Force Command. (*Forces Aériennes Stratégiques*)

After maintenance operations, the upper stage of the missile was transported in a container and then placed at the top of the missile. (*Armée de l'Air*)

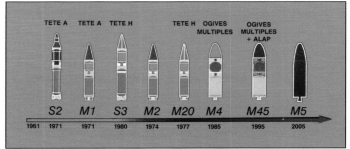

The history of French ballistic missiles: the S-2 and S-3 for *Plateau d'Albion* and the M-series of the strategic oceanic force. (Aerospatiale/ Arian Group).

The operation and navigation room of the submarine *Le Redoutable*. (Author's collection

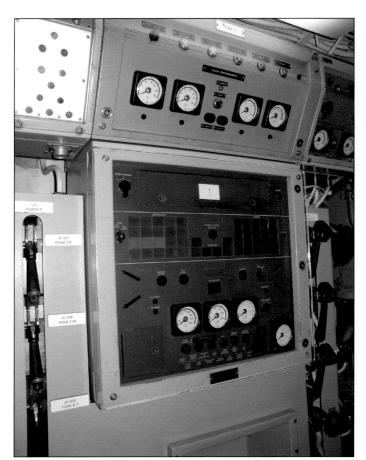

The control panel of one of the 16 missiles on *Le Redoutable*. (Author's collection)

A work station dedicated to the control of the nuclear reactor. (Author's photo)

set up the base, expropriation letters were signed by local farmers for compensation. A campaign against the project was launched in the local media, notably *La Marseillaise*, a left-wing newspaper. The facility and the operations carried out there were to be under the aegis of the French Air Force. On 25 August 1966, work began on the site, taking care to respect the natural beauty of the region. Nevertheless, silos and command rooms were designed to resist the effects of a nuclear strike. The base was divided into two groups of missiles, each controlled by a PCT (*Poste de Conduite de Tir*, or Fire Control Station) which was buried at a depth of 400m, one near the village of Rustrel and the other close to Reilhannette. In their concrete silos, the missiles were placed on platforms equipped with powerful shock absorbers. The doors over the silos weighed 145

tonnes. The distances between the silos was calculated to complicate a neutralization strike. Before their firing, the missiles were to be launched from their silos by explosives.

Missiles of the first generation, the S-2, were a two-stage solid-propulsion missile integrating a unique re-entry vehicle. With a range of 3,000km, the missiles were classed as IRBMs. Silos were dispersed and strongly hardened to reduce the effects of a direct nuclear attack. The *Plateau d'Albion* base was designed as a second strike force in relation to the concept of a defensive nuclear strategy. Each launching pad was a hardened silo where the missile was maintained in operational conditions, in order to be launched at very short notice – a matter of minutes. Aerospatiale was the

LE FIGARO — JEUDI 26 JUIN 1969

HIER, A QUELQUES KILOMÈTRES AU LARGE DE CHERBOURG

PREMIÈRE PLONGÉE STATIQUE DU « REDOUTABLE »

sous-marin à propulsion nucléaire destiné à la troisième génération de la force de dissuasion française

LE sous-marin *Le Redoutable* a effectué hier sa première plongée statique au large de Cherbourg, à 3 kilomètres des côtes environ. Commencée à 11 h 30, *Le Redoutable* refit surface à 18 h 37. Peu d'informations nous sont parvenues au sujet de cette première sortie en mer, l'état-major de la marine observant un mutisme absolu. Le sous-marin à propulsion nucléaire avait quitté hier matin, à 6 h 30, le mouillage sur coffre où il se trouvait à l'extrémité de la jetée du Homet pour gagner la baie du Becquet devant le petit port de Tourlaville.

Pour cette première sortie en mer, le premier sous-marin atomique français était escorté par plusieurs bâtiments de la marine nationale et un hélicoptère surveillait la zone où les essais se sont déroulés.

Cette nouvelle étape de la mise en service du *Redoutable* survient après sa prise d'autonomie nucléaire et aux essais au point fixe réalisés le mois dernier en rade de Cherbourg. Elle est destinée à vérifier l'étanchéité du sous-marin et à effectuer la « pesée » du navire.

C'est le capitaine de frégate Louzeau, premier pacha du sous-marin nucléaire, qui a dirigé et coordonné les manœuvres de cette plongée qui sera suivie dans quelques jours des essais de vitesse et de manœuvrabilité. Ces derniers auront lieu d'une part au large de Barfleur, d'autre part au nord des Casquets, c'est-à-dire respectivement à l'est et à l'ouest de la presqu'île du Cotentin.

Toutes précautions avaient été prises par la marine nationale pour éviter l'irruption, dans la zone des essais, de bateaux de commerce ou de pêche.

Premier des sous-marins nucléaires lance-engins balistiques à tête atomique, le *Redoutable* constituera avec ses successeurs immédiats le *Terrible* et le *Foudroyant* le troisième volet de la force de dissuasion française. La mise en chantier d'un quatrième puis d'un cinquième sous-marin est également prévue.

Long de 128 mètres, large de 10,6 m, d'un déplacement en surface de 8.000 tonnes, le *Redoutable* comporte à son bord vingt-neuf mille appareils divers, 250 km soit 130 tonnes de câblage électrique, 4 calculateurs, 4 périscopes aboutissant au « massif », cet immense parallélépipède, vital pour son électronique. Le réacteur à uranium enrichi provient de l'usine de Pierrelatte.

On sait que le *Redoutable* peut filer à plus de 20 nœuds (36 kilomètres à l'heure), à 300 mètres de profondeur et faire plus de quatre fois le tour de la Terre sans recharge de combustible.

Les 135 hommes de son équipage — tous des volontaires — vont se familiariser pendant des mois avec ce submersible qui, vers le milieu de l'année prochaine, recevra ses seize fusées à charge nucléaire — dont la puissance totale sera équivalente à près de 500 fois la bombe d'Hiroshima — et qui pourront être lancées à plus de 2.000 kilomètres.

Une fois tous les essais terminés, le *Redoutable* partira pour sa première croisière de trois mois sous les eaux sans faire surface.

AFRIQUE • AFRIQUE • AFRIQUE • AFRIQUE • AFR

A la veille de son rattachement officiel | En Afrique du Sud

In *Le Figaro*, the conservative daily newspaper, articles reported the milestones of the strike force programme, including the first test-diving of *Le Redoutable*. (Author's collection)

Giscard d'Estaing, France's newly elected president, took the decision to balance the place of nuclear forces in the national defence policy. The new economic situation of the 1970s did not, however, impede the arrival of a second generation of missiles, the S-3. The S-3 had better performance in terms of range and hardened protection of the warhead during the re-entry phase against enemy anti-ballistic missile (ABM) defences. In the wake of the ABM treaty between the USSR and USA, it was public knowledge that Moscow had been protected by the Galosh and Super Galosh systems. The S-3, in its new D configuration (meaning '*Durçi*', or 'Hardened'), integrates penetration improvements and a thermonuclear warhead with a yield of 1 megaton, a credible anti-demographic capability.

Deterrence from the sea: the first SSBN is christened Le Redoutable

Le Redoutable ushered in a class of six strategic submarines. Its name, as with all French SSBNs, was inspired by the tradition under the French monarchy of giving a name to all artillery pieces, bronze guns on which was inscribed the motto 'The king's last word', actually a close definition of modern deterrence. The vessel

main contractor, the state-owned company gathering several subcontractors: Sagem for the inertial navigation unit, and Crouzet, Sfena and Thomson for the electronics. The re-entry vehicle was designed by Aerospatiale and the warhead by the CEA. For tests and experiments, a specific silo able to conduct a series of launches was reserved at the *Centre d'Essais des Landes* near Biscarosse on the Atlantic coast with a target zone close to the Azores islands.

Each group of missiles was commanded and controlled by a highly protected underground launch room, connected to the Strategic Air Force headquarters by robust radio networks to guarantee the order coming from the President of the French Republic wherever his location. The first group of silos conducted a nuclear alert in 1971 and the second in 1972. At the same time, France's first nuclear strategic submarine conducted its inaugural strategic patrol. This breakthrough was the most significant upsurge of power in the military history of the nation. Sea-based missiles, plus *Plateau d'Albion*, made the strategic triad a reality. The diplomatic profit was immediate at the NATO level. A third group of nine silos was cancelled for economic reasons. In December 1974, Valery

also took the name of the warship from which the fatal bullet was fired that killed Admiral Nelson at the Battle of Trafalgar. The spirit of tradition has always been strong in '*La Royale*', the nickname of the French Navy under the Republic regime. Written in the Military Programming Law of 1960–1964, the decision to produce the first strategic submarine was signed on 2 March 1963. France took the option of an entirely sovereign development of its deterrence, the French SSBNs utilizing national technological resources. The stakes were so high that a dedicated organization was needed. Coelacanth was thus created within the new DMA – the armament directorate (the future DGA) – which closely oversaw the work entrusted to the DTCN (*Direction Technique Construction Navale*), acting as prime contractor. The conduct of the project took into account the lessons of Q244, a nuclear-powered attack submarine launched in the 1950s on the model of the USS *Nautilus* but halted for lack of technological maturity. Anticipating the future strategic vocation of the French naval forces, General de Gaulle declared at the Naval Academy in Brest on 15 February 1965: "The Navy now finds itself, and without doubt for the first time in its history, at the forefront

An M-4 missile in the integration facility of Aerospatiale, a picture taken during the 1980s. The missile entered in service on *L'Inflexible* in 1985, then equipped all of France's strategic submarines except *Le Redoutable*. (Aerospatiale/Arianegroup)

Tourville, an anti-submarine frigate. In the 1970s, the French MoD financed a significant force of anti-submarine frigates whose main mission was to protect the movements of the vessels of the Strategic Oceanic Force and to hunt *Marine Nationale* enemy submarines. In addition, a strong force of minesweepers was developed.

A launch of an M-4 type ballistic missile. The M-4 was the weapon that gave the French parity with their allies' submarines equipped with Poseidon or Trident, with multiple independent re-entry vehicles and a range of over 4,000km which extended significantly the areas of patrols in the Atlantic Ocean, a feature that reinforced the credibility of the *Force Océanique Stratégique*. (DGA)

of France's military power. In the future it will be every day more and more true." A key moment was the launch of the SSBNs on 29 March 1967, an occasion of majestic ceremony in the presence of Charles de Gaulle. Indeed, the general appreciated such a moment as it inaugurated the great achievements of his regime.

The challenge of nuclear propulsion

Unlike the American and Soviet roadmaps, which adopted a gradual approach – starting with a nuclear-powered attack vessel armed with torpedoes, followed by submarines armed with cruise missiles launched on the surface and even conventional diesel-electric subs carrying ballistic missiles – France worked on a comprehensive strategic concept: a direct path to a nuclear-powered submarine carrying strategic ballistic missiles launched underwater. The architecture of the SSBN was a copy of the US Navy's George Washington class of submarines (in service from 30 December 1959), with a missile section in the centre, between the central operation and propulsion areas, plus a torpedo room in the bow. Exploiting the legacy of large submarines, the vessels were manufactured at the Cherbourg arsenal. The main challenge was the nuclear propulsion. The solution chosen relied on a pressurized water reactor. This needed a prototype on land (PAT, *prototype à terre*), which was built by the CEA at its Cadarache research centre in Provence. Its construction was completed on 18 March 1960. Without waiting for the uranium produced by the Pierrelatte enrichment plant, the PAT was activated for the first time on 14 August 1964 thanks to enriched uranium supplied by the United States, a friendly gesture by Washington obtained as part of an agreement signed in 1959. In addition,

The launch ceremony of the *Améthyste*, the fifth in the class of French nuclear attack submarines, at Cherbourg on 14 May 1988, after four years of construction. The first SSN, *Le Rubis*, was launched on 7 July 1979. As the first in its class, the vessel needed over 1,000 hours of underwater testing before commissioning. *Le Rubis* commenced active service on 23 February 1983. Armed with torpedoes and SM-39 Exocet missiles, the SSN fleet gave better protection to France's strategic submarines and aircraft carriers. (DCN – Naval Group)

L'Inflexible, the sixth vessel of the Le Redoubtable class. Its construction began on 27 March 1980 and the vessel was launched on 23 June 1982; it was commissioned on 1 April 1985 and decommissioned on 14 January 2008. From 1985, the Strategic Oceanic Force (FOST) had a fleet of six SSBNs and could ensure deterrence through three ships at sea constantly, a capability of 48 ballistic MIRV (Multiple Independently targetable Re-entry Vehicle) missiles, each with six independent warheads. At the turn of the 1980s, the FOST had been hoisted to become the "diamond point of the deterrence force", as stated by President François Mitterrand.

the design of the propulsion section had been given by the American firm Westinghouse, but built by French industry. Three sailors, including one qualified as a nuclear engineer, ran the reactor. In the event of a shutdown of nuclear propulsion, the running of the ship relied on electric batteries and emergency diesel engines. In 1972, Admiral Louzeau, the first captain of *Le Redoutable*, commented: "There is also the technological challenge of the inertial under-sea navigation. We spent as much on the development of the inertial units as on the prototype of the nuclear propulsion."

Following the launch of *Le Redoutable* on 29 March 1967, work continued, its reactor being activated for the first time on 26 February 1969. On 2 July that year, it left the Cherbourg arsenal and headed north into the English Channel, making its first dive, when along with the crew were engineers who had taken part in the submarine's design. The training of submariners, officers and petty officers for this new submarine was provided by the Academy of Military Applications of Atomic Energy, a special school located in Cherbourg. In addition, a full-scale wooden model of the submarine in the arsenal at Cherbourg helped in the development of the prototype and made it possible to integrate modifications requested by the crew during evaluations at sea. In Brest, a simulator on land further helped the training of the crew. Others crew members were trained at civil nuclear plants. The vessel was a national priority, the budget necessary being sustained by the expansion of the French economy: around 5.3 percent on average during the 1960s. In the end, some 12 million hours of work were necessary for its completion. On 25 September 1970, operational service came a step nearer

CHERBOURG ARSENAL: SIX STRATEGIC MISSILE SUBMARINES IN ONE DECADE

In just two years, two sister ships of *Le Redoutable* entered service. *Le Terrible* was laid down on 24 April 1967. Launched on 12 December 1969, it joined the FOST operational patrol cycles on 1 January 1973, just one year after *Le Redoutable*. *Le Foudroyant* arrived quickly afterwards, on 6 June 1974. Laid down on 12 December 1969, it had been launched on 4 December 1971. A fourth SSBN, *L'Indomptable*, joined the French Navy on 23 December 1976. This submarine received 16 new M-20 missiles, a munition with a thermonuclear re-entry vehicle. Work on the M-20 had begun on 4 December 1971, with a launch at sea taking place on 19 September 1974. The series of SSBNs was reinforced by 'No 5', *Le Tonnant*, on 3 May 1980. Work on this began on 19 October 1974, the launch being carried out on 19 September 1977. The programme continued with a sixth SSBN, the *Inflexible*, which the navy arsenal put on hold on 27 March 1980. A fierce political debate between the President of the Republic, Valéry Giscard d'Estaing, a supporter of a fleet limited to five ships, and the National Assembly ruled by a neo-Gaullist majority, delayed the decision to finance this sixth SSBN. A decision to go ahead

was finally made on 25 September 1978 by the Defence Council, under the presidency of Giscard d'Estaing. Cancellation of this vessel would have been seen as an act of treason against the spirit of General de Gaulle. It is a risk that Giscard d'Estaing, the conservative president, did not want to take. It is also true that the fallout from the oil crisis of 1974 meant that the balance of finances became a major concern in France, as elsewhere, with the defence budget under pressure. On 23 June 1982, *L'Inflexible* was finally launched. It entered service on 1 April 1985 with 16 new MIRV M-4 missiles on board. In its national political aspect, the SSBN programme marked an affiliation between the right wing and socialists in nuclear affairs. The delay in the programme was an occasion to introduce several electronic innovations and better performances, a prelude to the forthcoming new generation concept that naval engineers were preparing for the next decade, when it would be necessary to replace the Redoutable class. *Le Redoutable* ended its operational career in 1991 after 58 operational patrols.

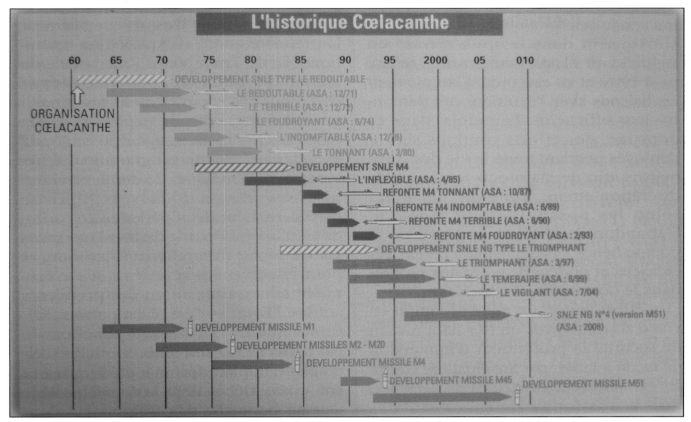

This chart gives details of the production programme and schedules of nuclear strategic submarines at the Cherbourg shipyards. (DGA)

when *Le Redoutable* left Cherbourg and headed for Brittany to the *Ile Longue* operational base. The integration of the ballistic missiles was the next milestone to be achieved. As part of the development of the first generation of missiles, the M1, four flight tests were achieved at the *Center d'Essais des Landes* and 15 from the *Gymnote* experimental submarine between 16 November 1968 and 5 May 1971. Just weeks later, on 29 May 1971, with the trajectory being controlled by the CEL, *Le Redoutable* carried out the first launch of a missile, followed by a second real test on 26 June. Observers noted the hydrodynamic masts, allowing surface observations at high-

speed periscopic immersion. The tactical situation was developed via a sonar from Sintra (now Thales). Precision was ensured by three Sagem inertial navigation units. Measurements could be readjusted by an astronomic aiming sight; located in the rear part of the PCNO, the central navigation and operations room, they were connected to the missile, thus allowing precision against the target.

The initial speartip of the French nuclear deterrent force was the Dassault Mirage IV strategic bomber: indeed, between 1964 and 1971, this was France's only means of delivering nuclear weapons. Envisaged as an aerially-refuellable platform right from the start, the Mirage IV was designed around the requirement to deliver a 3,000kg-heavy, 5.2-metres-long nuclear bomb over a range of 2,000km, while being able to reach supersonic speeds. Development began in 1957 and 62 were pressed into service between 1964 and 1968. They were deployed by a total of nine squadrons, each of which had a complement of four aircraft. They were operated in two pairs, each of which consisted of one aircraft carrying one nuclear bomb (initially an AN.11, then AN.22, and then AN.52) semi-recessed under the fuselage, and the other serving as a buddy-tanker. (Artwork by Tom Cooper)

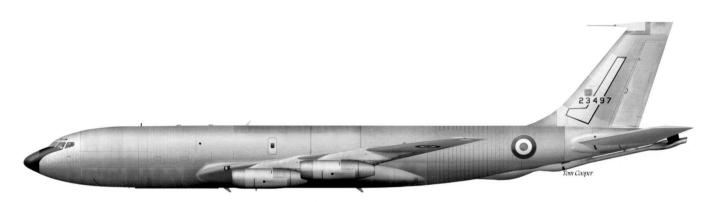

In reaction to the controversy over the fact that Mirage IVAs were on a 'one-way trip' when trying to reach some of their targets in the Soviet Union, the *Force de Dissuassion* decided to purchase 14 Boeing C-135FR tanker aircraft (12 active and 2 spares). Left in the same livery like KC-135As of the Strategic Air Command of the US Air Force – 'bare metal overall' – these were operated by ERV.3/93 Bretagne, ERV 4/31 Sologne, and ERV 4/91 Landes, starting from 1971. With their help, Mirage IVAs became capable of reaching targets over 3,500km away. This was the C-135FR 62-3497 (coded 31-CM). (Artwork by Tom Cooper)

While the complement of four aircraft per squadron was retained throughout the Mirage IVA's service, the actual alert status for most of the time included 36 bombers in operational condition: 12 ready to get airborne at short notice, 12 kept at four minutes readiness, and another 12 at 45 minutes readiness – all of them armed with a nuclear weapon. Initial attack profile was at high altitude and a speed of March 1.86. Before soon, the realisation that high-altitude operations were much too hazardous resulted in modifications for low-altitude penetration, although this reduced both the maximum speed and range. As a consequence, the aircraft received a livery in *Gris Bleu tres Fonce* (dark grey) overall, with a camouflage pattern in *Gris Vert Fonce* (dark green) on upper surfaces. Barrax electronic countermeasures pods (shown on outboard underwing pylon) were added in the late 1980s. (Artwork by Tom Cooper)

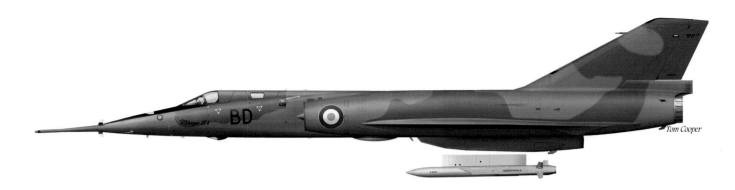

Powered by SNECMA Atar engines of 47kN (10,500lbs) thrust, and weighting about 32,000kg (70,000lbs) empty, the Mirage IVA had the maximum take-off weight of 64,000kg (140,000lbs) and could reach the speed of Mach 2.4 in clean configuration (usually reduced to Mach 2.2 due to airframe temperature restrictions). Combined with its very high operational altitude, this made it an excellent reconnaissance platform, leading to the creation of the Mirage IVR: modification of 12 aircraft to carry the CT.52 reconnaissance pod in the bomb recess. Each pod contained three or four long-range cameras: alternatively, an infrared line scanner could be installed. The insert shows an ASMP supersonic nuclear weapon, as added in the 1990s. (Artwork by Tom Cooper)

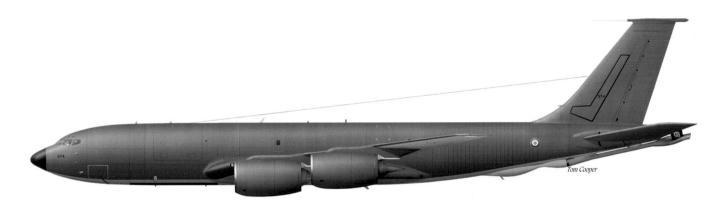

In the mid-1980s, 11 surviving C-135Fs were upgraded to the KC-135FR standard through the installation of CFM International F108 turbofan engines. Around the same time the fleet – meanwhile not only involved in Mirage IVA-operations, but also in supporting tactical fighter-bombers during French military interventions in the Central African Republic, Mauritania, and Chad – received this livery in blue grey (FS35164) on upper surfaces and sides, and either aluminium or light grey on undersurfaces. This was the KC-135FR serial number 62-3574 (coded 31-CP), while operated by ERV 93 Bretagne in Chad of 1986. (Artwork by Tom Cooper)

In April 1973, nuclear weapons were pressed into service with Dassault Mirage IIIE fighter-bombers of the EC 2/4 La Fayette squadron. Based on the Mirage IIIC interceptor, the IIIE was the multi-role and strike variant with an extended fuselage necessary for a larger avionics bay and an additional fuel tanks. Furthermore, it received a British-made Marconi continuous-wave Doppler navigation radar under the forward fuselage. The weapons system was centred on the Thomson-CSF Cyrano II dual mode radar, and the typical warload in the strike mission included a single AN.52 nuclear bomb installed under the centreline. Except for the EC 2/4, the sole other Mirage IIIE-unit equipped with such weapons was the EC 1/4 Dauphine. During the 1970s, their nuclear bombs were replaced by anti-radar missiles (right lower corner) (Artwork by Tom Cooper)

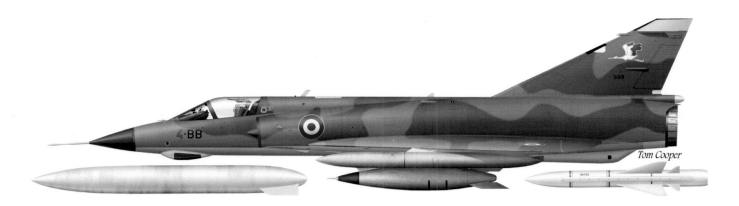

Nuclear-armed Mirage IIIEs were followed into service by SEPECAT Jaguar A. This was a twin-engined tactical fighter-bomber developed in cooperation between France and Great Britain, that entered service in 1973. Only a year later, EC 1/7 Provence was declared operational not only on the new jet, but also on the AN.52 nuclear bomb. The unit was followed by the EC. 3/7 Languedoc in 1975 (one of which aircraft as of 1981 is illustrated here), and the EC. 4/7 Limousin in 1981. Ironically, while Jaguars were never assigned to the Force de frappe, they had a task directly related to that of Mirage IVs: their duty was to 'clear the way' for nuclear-armed strategic bombers. Thus, once the AN.52 was withdrawn from service, in 1981, they were re-armed with anti-radar missiles and electronic warfare systems. (Artwork by Tom Cooper)

The Dassault Super Etendard was a carrier-borne strike aircraft developed to replace the ageing Dassault-Breguet Etendard IV. It entered service with the French Naval Aviation in 1978-1979: a total of 85 was built, equipping three units (11F, 14F, and 17F). On this type, the 4.2m long and 455kg heavy AN-52 was installed on its typical pylon but this was installed under the right wing, instead under the centreline. The warhead of the AN.52 was the same like that of the Pluton missile, and had two yield options: the low-yield (6-8kt), and the high-yield (25kt). Starting in 1992, the An.52 was replaced by ASMPs, as shown in inset. (Artwork by Tom Cooper)

The Mirage 2000N was originally planned to replace the older Mirage IVs, and custom tailored for the nuclear strike role from low altitude only. Based on the design of the Mirage 2000B two-seat conversion trainer, it was first flown in 1986, and entered service in 1988. The first sub-variant, 2000N-K1 (of which 30 were manufactured) was the last aircraft to enter service while still compatible with the AN.52. The ultimate sub-variant became the 2000N-K2, of which 45 were manufactured, and which was equipped with the ASAMP-A nuclear cruise missile, but also had the secondary conventional capability and a full defensive kit. (Artwork by Tom Cooper)

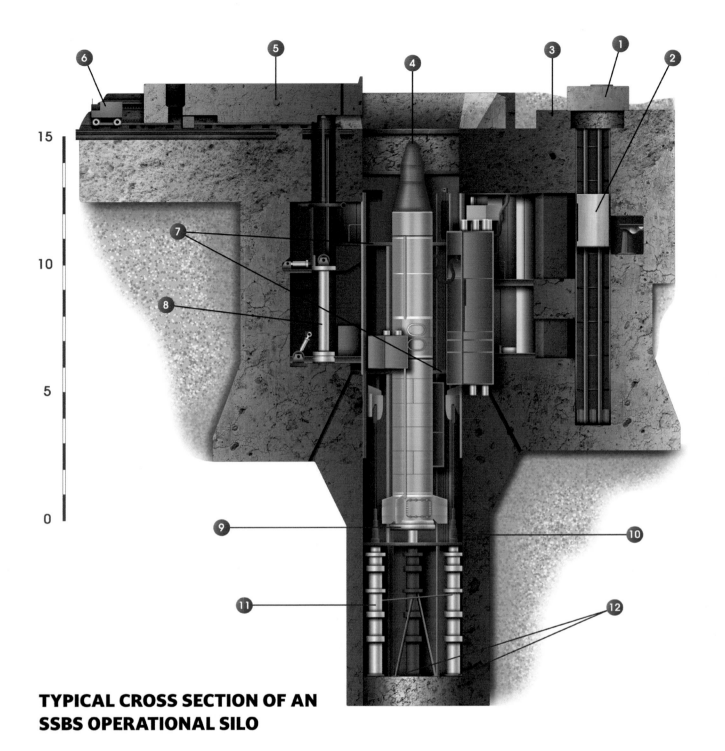

TYPICAL CROSS SECTION OF AN SSBS OPERATIONAL SILO

1. Reinforced concrete door
2. Personal lift
3. 26ft (8m) thick silo closure
4. Re-entry vehicle
5. Reinforced-concrete door
6. Door tug
7. Acess platforms
8. Counter-weights
9. Support ring
10. Cable/pulley suspension
11. Spring shock mounts
12. Anchorages for lowest platforms

(Artwork by Anderson Subtil)

The Pluton missile was a nuclear-armed tactical ballistic missile launched from a transporter erector launcher (TEL) based on the chassis of an AMX-30 tank. Designed to provide the tactical part of the French nuclear deterrence, it was 7m long and weighted 2,423kg on start, and had a range of between 17 and 120 kilometres, with a circular error probable of 150m. as far as is known, it could be equipped either with a warhead of 15kt or 25kt. The Pluton entered service in 1974, and was eventually operated by seven artillery regiments, assigned to the 1st, 2nd, and 3rd Army Corps', before the project was terminated in 1993. (Artwork by David Bocuqelet)

Designed to replace the Pluton, the Hadès was another inertially guided, short-range tactical ballistic missile. The work on this project began in 1975, with intention of deploying 120 weapons capable of reaching the range of 250km. Due to the end of the Cold War, the project was de-facto cancelled in 1991, when Paris took the decision not to deploy it. By 1993, 15 mobile launchers (illustrated here) and 30 missiles were ready: they were officially introduced to service but kept in storage for three years longer, when decommissioned and destroyed. The Hadès missile was equipped with a single nuclear warhead with a yield of 80kt. (Artwork by David Bocquelet)

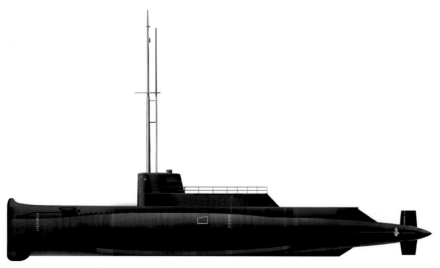

The *Gymnote* (S655) was an experimental submarine used for trials of submarine-launched ballistic missiles. The planned powerplant was to be a heavy water reactor, but with this not yet being ready, the vessel was equipped with diesel-electric propulsion: construction began in 1961, and *Gymnote* was commissioned with the hull number Q244 in 1966. Two years later, the vessel began running tests of M1 and M2 missiles. Following a major rebuild in 19787-1979, it served for testing of new M4 missiles, before receiving the final hull number S655. *Gymnote* was decommissioned in 1986. (Artwork by David Bocquelet)

LEFT Representing the second French attempt at constructing a nuclear-powered attack submarine, the *Rubis*-class represented the first generation of nuclear-powered attack submarines of the French Navy. A total of five boats were constructed to this design, including Rubis (S601; commissioned in 1983), Saphir (S602; 1984), Casabianca (S603; 1987), and Émeraude (S604; 1988), with a plan to construct four additional. Only 73.6m long, these were compact vessels displacing 2,400 tons when surfaced and 2,600 tons when submerged. Powerplant included a pressurised water reactor CAS-48, which could accelerate them to at least 25 knots (46km/h). As far as is known, their armament never included nuclear warheads: centred on four tubes calibre 533mm, it consisted of F17 mod2 guided torpedoes and SM.39 Exocet submarine-launched anti-ship missiles. (Artwork by David Bocquelet)

RIGHT Based on the design of the conventionally-powered *Agosta*-class, the first batch of two *Rubis*-class boats was plagued by high noise emissions. This resulted in a significant re-design, originally applied starting with the fifth vessel, which eventually became known as the *Amethyste*-class. Actually, all the earlier *Rubis*-class submarines were refitted to this standard, becoming virtually indistinguishable from each other. That said, four of the earlier vessels have experienced significant incidents in their careers and the one, *Saphir*, was taken out of service in 2019, followed by *Rubis* in 2022. Moreover, the last two planned boats (Turquoise and Diamant) were eventually cancelled. The resulting fleet of four SSNs now known as the Amethyste-class (including the namesake, hull-number S605, commissioned to service in 1992, and Perle, S606, commissioned in 1993, but also earlier and rebuilt Casabianca and Émeraude) is based in Toulon and forms the Nuclear-Powered Attack Submarine Squadron (Escadrille de sous-marins nucléaires d'attaque). (Artwork by David Bocquelet)

LEFT The *Le Redoutable*-class represented the first generation of French-designed and -constructed ballistic missile submarines (*Sous-marin Nucléaire Lanceur d'Engins*, SNLE; abbreviated with SSBN in English). A total of six vessels was constructed, including *Redoutable* (S611; commissioned in 1971), *Terrible* (S612; 1973), *Foudroyant* (S610; 1974), *Indomptable* (S613; 1976), *Tonnant* (S614; 1980), and *Inflexible* (S615; 1985), and all were meanwhile withdrawn from service. They had a length of 128m and were displacing up to 8,000 tons when submerged. The powerplant included one PWR reactor, and maximum speed was 'over 20 knots' (37km/h). Their armament initially included 16 M1 ballistic missiles with a range of 2,500km (1,600nm) and a single 400-kiloton warhead. In 1974, Foudroyant received the improved but heavier M2 missiles with a longer range and a 500-kiloton warhead. Eventually, both the M1 and the M2 were replaced by the M20. (Artwork by David Bocquelet)

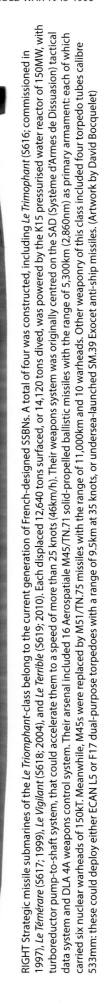

RIGHT Strategic missile submarines of the *Le Triomphant*-class belong to the current generation of French-designed SSBNs. A total of four was constructed, including *Le Triomphant* (S616; commissioned in 1997), *Le Téméraire* (S617; 1999), *Le Vigilant* (S618; 2004), and *Le Terrible* (S619; 2010). Each displaced 12,640 tons surfaced, or 14,120 tons dived, was powered by the K15 pressurised water reactor of 150MW, with turboreductor pump-to-shaft system, that could accelerate them to a speed of more than 25 knots (46km/h). Their weapons system was originally centred on the SAD (Système d'Armes de Dissuasion) tactical data system and DLA 4A weapons control system. Their arsenal included 16 Aerospatiale M45/TN.71 solid-propelled ballistic missiles with the range of 5,300km (2,860nm) as primary armament: each of which carried six nuclear warheads of 150kT. Meanwhile, M45s were replaced by M51/TN.75 missiles with the range of 11,000km and 10 warheads. Other weaponry of this class included four torpedo tubes calibre 533mm: these could deploy either ECAN L5 or F17 dual-purpose torpedoes with a range of 9.5km at 35 knots, or undersea-launched SM.39 Exocet anti-ships missiles. (Artwork by David Bocquelet)

SOUS-MARIN NUCLÉAIRE LANCEUR D'ENGINS
TYPE "LE REDOUTABLE - M4"

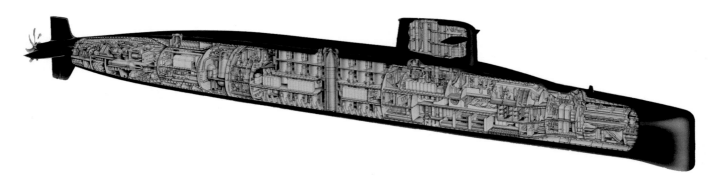

A cross-section of a vessel of the *Le Redoutable*-class – a series of six vessels that represented the first generation of French-designed and -constructed SSBNs. While the resulting French fleet was of similar size to that of the British Royal Navy, contrary to Great Britain, France received no support from any other nations, and had to develop every piece of related equipment – including nuclear reactors, but also high-tensile steel – entirely from the scratch. The same was valid for ballistic missiles and nuclear warheads installed on this class. (DCNS)

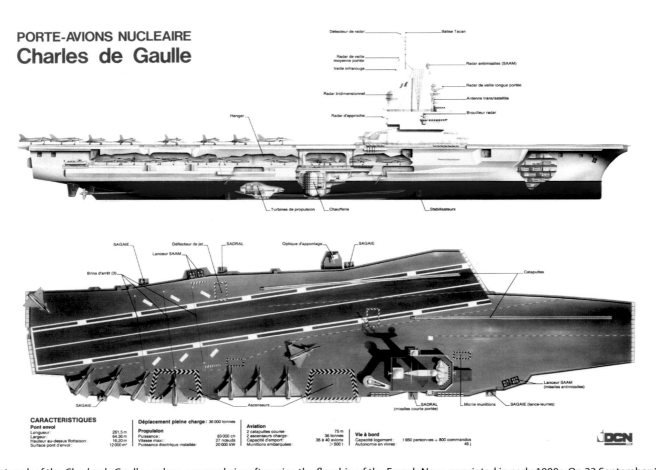

An artwork of the *Charles de Gaulle* nuclear-powered aircraft carrier, the flagship of the French Navy, as printed in early 1990s. On 23 September 1980, the Defence Council decided to build two nuclear carriers, but due to the lack of funding and economic recession of the early 1990s, the construction was eventually limited to just one. The hull was laid down at the DCNS naval shipyard in Brest, in April 1989, and launched in May 1994: originally to be named *Richelieu*, the vessel was commissioned into service under the name *Charles de Gaulle*, on 18 May 2001, becoming the largest warship constructed in Western Europe since 1950. Based in Toulon, the ship is displacing 42,500 tons at full load. It is equipped with two steam catapults, and an air wing including a total of 36 Dassault Rafale fighter-bombers (armed with, between others, ASMP-A nuclear missiles), Grumman E-2C Hawkeye early warning aircraft, and Aerospatiale/Eurocopter AS.365F Dauphin Pedro, EC.725 Caracal, and AS.532 Cougar combat-search- and rescue helicopters. For self-defence purposes, *Charles de Gaulle* is armed with four 8-cell AS-43 Sylver launchers for MBDA Aster surface-to-air missiles, two 6-cell Sadral launchers for Mistral short-range surface-to-air missiles, and up to eight Giat 20F2 cannons calibre 20mm (replaced by three Nexter Narwhal guns, in 2018). The carrier meanwhile made more than a dozen of cruises, primarily in the Mediterranean Sea and the Indian Ocean, and took part in combat operations in Afghanistan, Libya, and Syria. (DCNS)

GYMNOTE

A testbed ship, *Gymnote*, played its part in the construction and modernization of the Strategic Oceanic Force. The vessel was a refurbishment of a hull produced in the 1950s within the project of a nuclear-propelled submarine. The ship kept the number of its hull: Q244. At that time, using natural uranium technology for propulsion, French engineers had been unable to produce a reactor compact enough to fit into the ship, difficulties which led to the cancellation of the project in 1959. The DGA, the French armament directorate, took up the Q244 hull, which was in reserve, and redesigned the vessel for experimentation regarding the main deterrent systems on board submarines.

Design works were entrusted to armaments engineer André Gempp, who also designed the FNRS 3 Bathyscaphe scientific submarine, the diesel-electric Daphne-class submarines and the *Le Redoutable*. The ship was christened *Gymnote* (code name S655). Launched on 17 March 1964, it entered service on 17 October 1966. Its inelegant silhouette was recognizable by its short platform behind the kiosk, encapsulating four tubes. Diesel-electric propulsion would be sufficient to voyage offshore to perform launches or tests. Propulsion was via Pielstick 12PA2 engines driving two lines. *Gymnote* was no race-car at sea: just 10 knots on the surface, 11 knots when diving. The vessel had no torpedo tubes. Its mission focused on the last sequence of the development of missiles: the M-1, M-20, then the MIRV M-4. Its operational life was busy, with engineers on board for the conducting of tests. The first test of the M-1 was carried out on 19 April 1967; six others would follow the same year. Between 1976 and 1978, the submarine received structural modifications to accommodate the larger M-4 tubes. On 10 March 1982, it conducted his first M-4 test. The last launch took place on 22 February 1984. The *Gymnote* carried out a total of 136 launch sequences in the Mediterranean or the Atlantic Ocean. This platform also contributed to the development of work stations, optronic masts and inertial navigation systems: the CIN M-1 and then CIN M-2 units from Sagem. The *Gymnote* was decommissioned on 1 October 1986 andscrapped at Saint-Nazaire in 1996.

Gymnote, off the coast near Toulon. In this image, we can see the aft platform and its four vertical silos. The vessel had a length of 84m and a displacement of 3,250 tons in full load. The crew included eight officers. (*Marine Nationale*)

First strategic patrol

On 7 July 1971, *Le Redoutable* completed its TLD (long-duration mission), the 54-day sortie being the final milestone before the vessel was admitted to active service. Admiral Louzeau recalled:

> When after three days at sea, we realized that we no longer needed to go back to the surface, it was extraordinary! For this navigation, the missiles were not loaded with their atomic charge. The trials allowed the crews of submariners to rotate, and thus allowed me to train two crews with a single vessel, since we had chosen to form two crews per vessel on the US Navy model. The year 1971 was the hardest for me, because I had the mission to

bring my ship into active service, while training the crews. To form the crews, I made the selection with Commander Buisson, my colleague in charge of the second deterrence patrol at sea.

On 15 January 1972, the day of *Le Redoutable*'s first operational patrol, the French strategic posture took on a new dimension, with a second strike capability from the sea. The nuclear submarine's departure took place in the presence of the Chief of Staff of the Armed Forces and the Chief of Operations of the French Navy. Armed with two crews, one named Red and the other Blue (Starboard and Port in Royal Navy parlance), the submarine thereafter carried out strategic missions for an average of 70 days. Some patrols included

PIERRES PRÉCIEUSES (OR GEMSTONES): AN ACADEMY OF MISSILES FOR DETERRENCE AND SPACE STRATEGY

Back in the 1960s, *Agate*, *Topaze*, *Rubis*, *Saphir*, *Émeraude* and *Diamant* were a series of experimental rockets that made it possible to design the strategic strike force. Their poetic names – all gemstones, or *Pierre précieuses* – were given to the missiles by Lieutenant-Colonel Jean Bedel, an air force officer assigned to the Hammaguir test range in Algeria. After the Liberation of France in 1944, rocketry was regarded by the French armed forces as a revolution in military affairs, a way to restore their martial power. When the military nuclear programme was decided upon at the end of the 1950s, France was far from the level reached in such matters by the Americans and Soviets, but its engineers did not have to start completely from scratch. The French ballistic adventure had humble beginnings in the form of sounding rockets. The V-2 rocket of von Braun served as the basis for the Véronique rocket, designed at the LRBA in Vernon with the help of German engineers who had taken refuge in France. Indeed, in 1945, the French military secret service had brought back home a V-2, German rocket engines and drawings. Their first achievement owed a lot to Dr Heinz Bringer, chief designer of the V-2's propulsion in Peenemünde within the teams under Wernher von Braun. After the capitulation of the Reich, he found refuge in France with 50 of his colleagues. This group proved an unexpected prize. Integrated into the French work in the rocketry field, the Germans gave their counterparts all that they knew about missile technology. They were then free to go back to Germany. Heinz Bringer decided to stay, having no family in Germany. He would prove to be essential to the development of the European Ariane launcher.

The origins of the French ballistic missile programme dates back to 1946, when the LRBA (Laboratoire de recherches balistiques et aérodynamiques) was created in Vernon, 70km west of Paris on the Normandy border, to develop military or civilian rockets, taking advantage of the V-2. Within just a decade, between the programme of 1960 and missiles coming into operation, a national ballistic force was up and running. In comparison, adopting a different path, the British government maintained limited efforts

The series of *Pierres précieuses* rockets began with *Agate*. The experimental rocket had a length of 8.50m, a diameter of 0.80m and a mass of 3.2 tonnes. The *Agate* was used to test instrument capsules and recovery systems. (LRBA Photo; DGA)

Based on the German V-2, Véronique was the first Western European liquid-fuel research and sound rocket. Véronique was a contraction of Vernon-électronique, and was also a French female first name, a new tradition in the domain that eventually led to Ariane, the European space launcher. Before being based in French Guiana, France's space launches were made in Colomb-Béchar and Hammaguir in Algeria. (LRBA Photo; DGA)

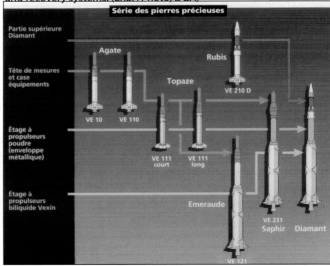

As detailed in this chart, the 'gemstones' rockets programme was a roadmap of technological demonstrators that built up a new expertise to successfully produce the missiles of the *Force de frappe*. The programme also had a civil dimension to address the market of commercial access to space. (LRBA Photo; DGA)

Topaze was developed and produced by Sereb, a joint venture composed of Nord Aviation and Sud Aviation. (LRBA Photo; DGA)

The *Rubis* featured a two-stage design, by using *Agate* for its first stage. The *Rubis* had a diameter of 0.80m and a length of 9.60m. The *Rubis* was launched 11 times from 10 June 1964 to 5 July 1967. (DGA)

on heavy bombers, utilizing its budgets on the V series – Valiant, Vickers and Vulcan. Exploiting encouraging early results, a French civil launcher was decided upon on 18 December 1960. By setting up a dual sector from the beginning through to the development phase, France was taking the path already explored by the Soviets and Americans, as demonstrated by the successful Semiorka and Atlas programmes. From the outset, France demonstrated an unfailing political will, mobilizing an army of engineers and other personnel working within an agile organization. The teams moved quickly from the drawing board to prototypes. The philosophy of the series of rockets was to entrust each type with the exploration of a specific technical domain. The 'gemstones' proved to be an academy for learning and exploring the technologies of a space launcher, from propulsion to materials, stage separation, piloting electronics, inertial navigation, telemetry and system integration, all of which had to be able to operate in an extreme environment.

The LRBA at Vernon had a hypersonic wind tunnel and developed the propulsion and design of the navigation system, all in cooperation with the DGA Propulsion test centre. Management of the missiles was entrusted to Sereb, a state-owned company created on 17 September 1959. In April 1961, the management opted for solid propulsion, a choice motivated by operational considerations. Indeed, delegations had been invited officially to the US to see the Atlas ICBM operations in their launch pads, noting the complexity and risks of the launch sequence using liquid propulsion. At the Bouchet research centre, the first propellants were developed, the *Ecole Polytechnique* providing its computer, an instrument that was unique in France.

Agate, the first vehicle, allowed, from 1961, the validation of the propulsion system, the separation of the re-entry vehicle and the telemetry systems. Eight tests were carried out. Then there was *Topaze*, which on its first flight in December 1962 was used to study the piloting devices of the nozzles. *Topaze* recorded 13 successes out of 14 flights, the last two being used to test the inertial navigation system. The separation of the stages and the piloting by orientation of nozzles was validated with *Émeraude*. This new vehicle was more ambitious, with its diameter increasing from 80cm to 1.4m. The results were exploited by the two-stage *Saphir* and *Diamant*, which were used to design the re-entry vehicles where the atomic payload would take place. From 1965, engineers moved on to the development of the operational missiles. Between 1965 and 1972, 27 development tests were conducted for the ground-to-ground system (prototypes were named S-112, S-01 and S-02) and 28 for the oceanic missiles (M-112 and M-011/012/013). Both shared the same propulsion stage. For the civil space launcher, officials of the DMA began to cooperate with CNES, the National Centre for Space Studies, which had just been created on 1 March 1962 and is still operational in the 2020s. To

Continued on page 46

Continued from page 45

Diamant was the first French expendable launch system and the first launcher not built by either the United States or USSR. (Aerospatiale)

obtain rapid results, *Diamant* was modified. Six missions were achieved with *Diamant*, including four successful ones between June 1964 and June 1965. At Hammaguir on 26 December 1965, *Diamant* launched Asterix, the first French satellite, into orbit. Its name had been chosen by the programme's managers as a tribute to the popular Gallic cartoon hero. The associated media campaign was also a success. After the USSR and USA, France thus became the third power to be in space. Newly elected in 1974, President Valéry Giscard d'Estaing decided in 1975 to halt the evolution of

Lift-off for a *Diamandt*A1 space launcher from Hammaguir on 26 November 1965, which had as its mission to put into orbit Asterix, the first French satellite. (LRBA/Arianegroup)

Diamant, believing it had reached its limits, and instead initiated the more ambitious European Ariane project.

firing exercises, with up to four missiles in one salvo. Three types of missiles would follow one another aboard, with three major upgrades. From August 1974 to April 1975, the vessel received the new M-2 missile and a reload of the reactor. Between August 1979 and March 1981, the ship went back for a second reload of the reactor and associated work to receive the new M-20, a missile that it would keep until the end of its service. Finally, in April 1985, *Le Redoutable* was out of action for 17 months in order to once again proceed with the reloading of the reactor.

During patrols, the crew could enjoy levels of comfort that had been raised to the highest standard for this class of combat ship: air regeneration, individual bunks, large dining rooms, fresh water, showers, sport equipment, a relaxation area and clean working conditions thanks to nuclear propulsion. The area surrounding the 16 missile tubes was used by the crew for jogging. A fully equipped medical room was manned by a doctor (with dental qualifications), an anaesthetist and a male nurse. By French tradition, the ship had

its own bakery producing fresh bread daily – and croissants on Sundays. Marine traditions were respected on board: 'President of the diner', tablecloth and silverware for officers' lunch and dinners.

During the first years of the vessel's service, the escort at the departure from *l'Île Longue* was carried out by the Agosta class, the most advanced French diesel-electric submarines. This protection was significantly enhanced by the new nuclear attack submarines of the Rubis class. These were also very useful to train officers and crews of the strategic submarine force. Due to their similar features, their arrival opened up a new period of cooperation with the United Kingdom and USA, other nations with nuclear attack submarines. The missiles force was funded by a significant budget, which represented more than 20 percent of the national defence expenditure in 1990. Dedicated to a unique mission, that of nuclear deterrence, the submarine force gained strong political support, an advantage when ushering in the uncertainties of the 1990s.

PLATEAU D'ALBION: A 'NO FUTURE' OPTION

The *Plateau d'Albion* was a subject of debate for a long time due to its vulnerability to a nuclear attack. According to the official doctrine, the fortress was regarded as part of France's vital interests, so a strike by nuclear weapons on its silos could have justified a nuclear retaliation by its bombers or submarines. The question of its modernization arose in 1980. Several options were studied, including a new missile in the existing base, actually the S-4 missile or one derived from the oceanic missile. Another option was a mobile system in a truck. This solution, known as 'SX', was subsequently designated S-45. This was President Jacques Chirac's preferred solution. Lastly, there was the option of dismantling the *Plateau d'Albion*. In a speech at the military school in front of members of the High Institute for National Defence Studies on 11 September 1988, François Mitterrand decided to reject the mobile missile force, dubbed '*missiles à roulettes*', which had echoes of the term 'bombinette'. The end of the programme was now in sight. The geopolitical changes in Europe in November 1989, with the fall of communism, speeded up the decision, which was eventually taken on 13 June 1995 by the newly elected Jacques Chirac. In view of the strategic context, its cost-effectiveness no longer justified its place in the Strike Force. On 16 September 1996, the operational alert of the *Groupement de Missile Stratégiques* ended definitively after 25 years. Its missiles had featured an operational availability of 98 percent (the other 2 percent representing periods of maintenance). The missiles from the Saint-Christol base can now be seen in a permanent exhibition at the Air and Space Museum at Le Bourget.

Inside the command post of one of the two strategic missile groups at *Plateau d'Albion*. (Photo *Armée de l'Air*)

An S-3 missile inside the maintenance workshops at *Plateau d'Albion*. (*Armée de l'Air*)

5
TACTICAL NUCLEAR CAPABILITY WITH STRATEGIC VISION

A speech given on 23 November 1961 by General de Gaulle, President of the *Ve Republique*, affirmed the need for tactical nuclear units. The plan was written in the 1964–70 programme law with the task of replacing the US atomic systems deployed by French forces: the Honest John missiles and the F-100 Super Sabres armed with Mk-28 bombs. The fission payloads would be developed by the CEA. This force encompassed five air force squadrons (two on Mirage IIIs, three on Jaguars) and five artillery regiments with Pluton missiles. In addition, the aircraft carriers *Clemenceau* and *Foch* were upgraded to house nuclear bombs. The air-delivered weapon was the AN-52, which would share the same core as the Pluton missile, officially named *Charge tactique commune*, or CTC. The technologies produced for this force had positive effects on France's conventional units, encouraging electronic warfare, multi-source intelligence, secured information, training, targeting, and the combination of conventional manoeuvres and nuclear raids. In the air force, the creation of Fatac, or *Force aérienne tactique*, in 1965 was a direct result of the decision to quit the integrated command of NATO. Fatac was in addition a deep renewal of the air force, with the intention of reaching the technological level of the Strategic Air Force.

A strategic vision for tactical nuclear weapons

The purpose of this nuclear arsenal was firstly diplomatic: to set up a sovereign force for a scenario of war in Europe. Its development inked the emancipation of the French armies in Europe regarding NATO and the willingness to defend French territory. General de Gaulle insisted that France would conduct a war in a way chosen at the Elysée palace. France rejected an invitation to join the Nuclear Planning Group. To reinforce deterrence, the tactical nuclear

forces sent a clear message to the enemy, before the strategic level. Whether or not these weapons were designed for battle, they were the first step into a strategic space. General Charles Ailleret, chief of staff, wrote in *Défense Nationale* in 1965: "[I]f the battle begins, the side which will be deprived of nuclear weapons will be struck with total powerlessness against the army possessing these weapons. [...] as soon as we are provided with the armament capable of striking

Based on a US Army map, this is an illustration of the expected principal axes of attack into West Germany by the Warsaw Pact armies in Central Europe. (Map by Anderson Subtil)

The training device of the AN-52 tactical bomb. The first unit was delivered to the French Air Force in 1972. The weapon had a length of 4.25m and weighed 680kg. Its plutonium core was able to produce a yield of 25 kilotons. (Photo by author)

hard and far, we will have weapons intended to participate in the close battle."

In 1974, Valéry Giscard d'Estaing, elected after the death of President Pompidou, wanted to rebuild a new relationship with Washington. Not a Gaullist, d'Estaing suggested an evolution of the radical vision of General de Gaulle and Georges Pompidou. To set up his diplomatic line of contact, he established positive personal relations with US President Gerald Ford. Tactical nuclear weapons were part of a new French strategic concept, offering a wider sanctuary and new relations with the allies. This choice had an effect on the nuclear programmes, due to a new need for long-range strikes. This operational aspect was also in line with the idea of d'Estaing to found a special relationship with Helmut Schmidt, the social democrat Chancellor of West Germany. Actually, Bonn was not very comfortable with nuclear raids coming from German soil (including the DDR). As a result, d'Estaing promoted nuclear tactical aviation (the Pluton missile has a range of 120km, whereas the Jaguar can fly over 3,000km). In addition, the CEA was encouraged to develop the neutron payload, the weapon of choice to stop armoured divisions. As a result, he received harsh criticism from Jacques Chirac and his party, the new position being read as a notch in the Gaullist doctrine. In the orthodox vision, the acceptance of a nuclear battle in Europe meant that nuclear deterrence had failed. On 10 July 1975, the French president met US Secretary of State Henry Kissinger and suggested a coordination between French forces and those of NATO, including in the domain of tactical nuclear weapons. The issue was not one of pure theory. General Jean Méry, the French chief of staff, met General Alexander Haig, commanding officer at SHAPE (Supreme Headquarters Allied Powers Europe), about coordination, notably targeting. Nevertheless, Paris retained its liberty. The options promoted by d'Estaing were seen, however,

A Pluton missile of the French Army during a training launch. An internal guidance system comprising an inertial unit ensured the required precision on impact. Its range was about 120km. (DGA Photo)

as presenting the risk of a potential integration of French nuclear forces in the disarmament talks between the USA and USSR. The diplomatic atmosphere of 1966 was now just a bad memory.

A Jaguar of EC 1/7 Provence Squadron equipped with an AS-37 Martel anti-radar missile. Electronic warfare and suppression of enemy air defence was becoming a priority for the French Air Force to support the nuclear deterrence mission of the *Force aérienne tactique*. The Jaguar units demonstrated their credibility in several overseas operations, from Africa in the 1970s to Kuwait in 1991. (DGA Photo)

This strike would be a 'final warning' before the escalation to strategic weapons. Any nuclear weapons, whatever their type, had a strategic dimension in this approach of strategy. A second generation was in preparation in the 1970s, an effort that produced the Mirage 2000, ASMP air-to-ground missile and Hades mobile system. A synergy of technologies provided the missile's direction: the ASMP (then ASMP-A) could conduct either pre-strategic nuclear missions or long-range strategic raids as retaliation for a nuclear attack against France.

Mirage IIIE: the first multi-role fighter-bomber

In the wake of the operational success of the Mirage IIIC, Dassault turned its attention towards a strike variant of the aircraft integrating a multi-mission system. The Mirage IIIE was the first nuclear tactical bomber of the French nuclear strike force, the aircraft being equipped with the AN-52 atomic bomb. The new version featured a Thomson-CSF Cyrano II dual-mode radar combining air-to-air and terrain-following functions. This variant remained in a single-seat configuration. On 5 April 1961, the first aircraft of a batch of three prototypes made its first flight. The aircraft had a 12-inch extra section just behind the cockpit, an extension needed to house the larger avionics bay. In addition, the new fuselage had a bigger fuel capacity, but did not receive a refuelling probe. A radar warning receiver was added in the vertical tail, while a Barax jamming pod by Electronic Serge Dassault could be mounted under the wing. On 14 January 1964, the first production Mirage IIIE was delivered. In October 1972, the 4th Fighter Squadron at Luxeuil in eastern France received its first AN-52s, making it the first operational Fatac unit with nuclear capability. Some of the aircraft had an anti-radar mission, in order to create paths of penetrations for the nuclear raids. SEAD (Suppression of Enemy Air Defences) was ensured with the AS-37 Martel missile, which was fixed in the same place as the nuclear bomb. The AS-37 Martel was the result of a cooperation with British engineers. In this configuration, Mirage IIIEs could be tasked to escort Mirage IVs for their strategic raids. These EW pods contributed to the modernization of the *Force Aérienne Stratégique* and the Super Étendard squadrons of the French Navy.

The nuclear capability of the Mirage IIIE was tested in the Pacific, for which an aircraft of the 2/4 La Fayette Squadron was chosen. The nuclear status of the Mirage III boosted its international interest. All nations looking for a nuclear military capability, or expecting one, considered the aircraft as a surrogate solution to a bigger platform, such as the Mirage IV, which was not cleared for export markets. Israel, as well as South Africa, Pakistan and Switzerland, selected the Mirage IIIE for its comprehensive capabilities.

Jaguar: a cooperation across the Channel

The features of the Jaguar can be compared to those of the A-4 Skyhawk or the A-7 Corsair. Its launch was the result of a convergence of British and French needs for an advanced trainer. On

A Jaguar surrounded by its panoply of conventional weapons. In the centre is the AN-52 tactical nuclear bomb. (Photo by Yves Le Mao/*Armée de l'Air*)

The ultimate decision for a nuclear engagement, including the use of tactical weapons, remained in the hands of the President of the Republic, and to him alone. The concept was refined in the 1980s: François Mitterrand, the socialist president elected in May 1981, gave an exclusive pre-strategic posture to the aircraft and Pluton regiments to be executed with tactical nuclear weapons.

FIGHTER SQUADRONS ARMED WITH AN-52 TACTICAL NUCLEAR BOMB

April 1973	EC 2/4 La Fayette	Mirage IIIE
November 1973	EC 1/4 Dauphiné	Mirage IIIE
September 1974	EC 1/7 Provence	Jaguar
July 1975	EC 3/7 Languedoc	Jaguar
July 1981	EC 4/7 Limousin	Jaguar

A Mirage IIIE of the La Fayette Squadron. The aircraft was tasked for a live test in the Pacific test range on 28 August 1973. (Hervé Beaumont's collection)

Another nuclear-capable tactical fighter-bomber of Fatac was this Mirage IIIE of the EC 2/2 Champagne Squadron. The aircraft is equipped with a Barax ECM pod. (Dassault Electronique, now Thales)

July 2005. The Jaguar also had a SEAD capability through BOA pods and AS-37 Martel missiles. The unit was operational from 1977 within the 3/3 Ardennes Squadron, with a mission to clear the path for Fatac fighters or Mirage IVs. As in the Royal Air Force, the *Armée de l'air* Jaguars paved the way for a revolution in precision guided munitions. The aircraft was well adapted to integrate the new Atlis optronic pod developed by Thomson-CSF for the delivery of the AS-30 Laser air-to-ground missile and Matra laser-guided bombs. In this conventional configuration, the Jaguar headed to Al Asra base in Saudi Arabia to be part of Operation *Desert Storm* in January and February 1991.

In an equivalent version, RAF Jaguar squadrons eventually carried the WE-177 nuclear bomb. The last nuclear training flight was carried out on 23 August 1991 by the A26 aircraft, with Colonel Barret, commander of 1/7 Provence, in the cockpit.

Pluton missiles: forward battle in the north and the east

In 1964, the French Army, being a strong partner in the Atlantic Alliance, was tasked to deploy the Honest John nuclear rocket. This special cooperation

the British side, the project was defined by Air Staff Target 362. The French requirement was called ECAT, *École de Combat et d'Appui Tactique*, for an advanced supersonic trainer. A Memorandum of Understanding was signed in May 1965 which led to the setting-up of Sepecat, *Société Européenne de Production de l'Avion d'École de Combat et d'Appui Tactique* ('European Company for the Production of a Combat Trainer and Tactical Support Aircraft'). In 1966, a joint venture between Breguet and the British Aircraft Corporation was signed to develop and produce the aircraft. The French Air Force took delivery of the first series copy in 1973, one of a fleet of 160 single-seat Jaguars. France also took 40 of the two-seat Jaguar Es. The system combining the Jaguar with the AN-52 was validated during the Maquis test conducted on 25 July 1974 from the Pacific Experimentation Centre. The weapon produces a yield of 20 kilotons.

On 6 April 973, the first nuclear alert was taken by the Mirage IIIEs of the 2/4 La Fayette Squadron, followed by the Jaguars of 1/7 Provence on 1 September 1974. The first unit to welcome the Jaguar, the 1/7 Provence was also the formation of the French Air Force which kept it fleet the longest, until its withdrawal from service on 1

with the US Army could be considered as a nuclear academy for the French artillery regiments. The Pluton mobile ground-to-ground weapon replaced the Honest John. Its mission was the same from an operational point of view, the Pluton being tasked to target Soviet armoured brigades. The programme moved fast, the development being endorsed by the President of the French Republic during a Defence Council held on 10 November 1966. The first test was carried out on 25 January 1968 at the Landes Test Centre. Like all nuclear forces, the Pluton could only be fired by order of the President of the Republic. Its management was the responsibility of Aerospatiale, now a component of Airbus. It was an integration of a solid-propelled single-stage piece carrying a single nuclear payload. The nuclear core was common to the AN-52. The SEP corporation developed the propulsion, Sfena the equipment, CII and Cintra the C3 functions and Sagem the navigation system. This precision piece of engineering integrated three inertial units coupled to a computer, to prevent the triggering of the payload in the event of drift from the planned route. Giat provides the vehicle, a tracked platform derived from the recovery version of the AMX-30 main battle tank.

A Jaguar in a training flight over France with a training AN-52. The aircraft conducted a live nuclear test on 25 July 1974. Under the left wing can be seen a Barracuda ECM pod. (Photo by Yves le Mao/ *Armée de l'Air*)

An SA-8 Gecko short-range missile system at the Threat training facility of Nellis Air Force Base, Nevada. The range of the missile was 12km. With its NATO allies, France developed the Mace and Embow electronic warfare trials to have better self-defence systems on its military aircraft. (Photo by author)

The SA-3 Goa missile system, a credible medium-range weapon of the Warsaw Pact with a range of 30km. Considering the lessons learnt in Vietnam by the US air forces and in the Six Days War, synergies were set up on threats and self-protection between the electronic warfare officers of Fatac and the FAS for the benefit of all services and forces, notably the navy and army aviation. (Photo by author)

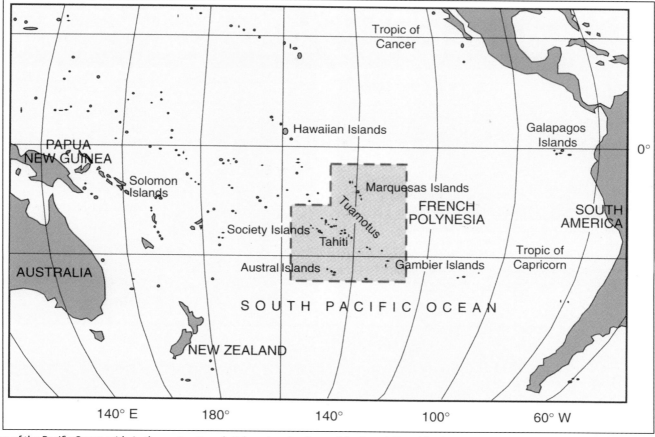

A map of the Pacific Ocean with, in the centre, French Polynesia, a territory of the French Republic. (AIEA)

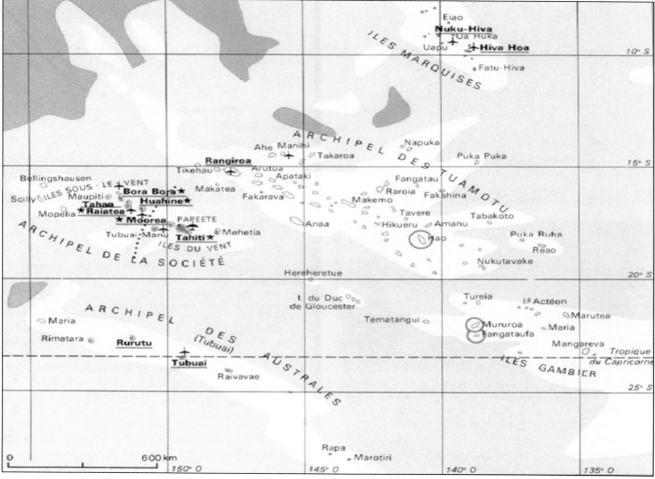

On this map of French Polynesia, three atolls of the Pacific test range are marked with red circles: Hao, Fangataufa and Mururoa. (CEA)

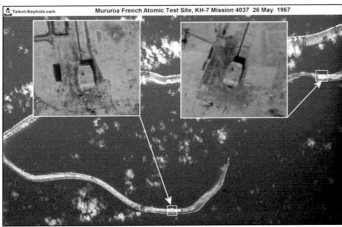

A picture of the reinforced concrete bunkers on Mururoa island, shot by a Key Hole satellite operated by the US intelligence community. These bunkers were built to monitor the atmospheric nuclear tests. (US DoD)

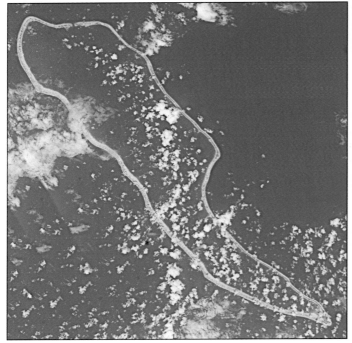

The atoll of Hao, one of the islands that the CEP transformed for the stand-off support of nuclear tests. (NASA)

Mururoa, 12 July 1966: 5H34, the ignition of *Aldebaran*, the first atomic test conducted by the CEP. Under the protection of the *Foch* aircraft carrier, the device produced 28 kilotons of energy over Mururoa. Radioactive fallout was thereafter detected on Mangaréva island and atoll of Totegegie. (CEA)

- 34 payloads were suspended from tethered balloons (31 at Mururoa and three at Fangataufa).

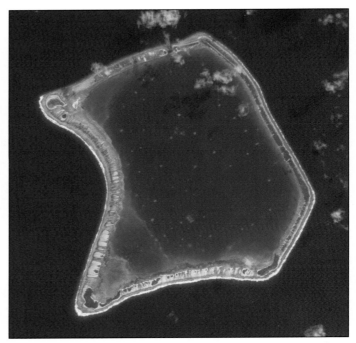

Fangataufa (22° 15′ S, 138° 45′ W), viewed in 2005 from a NASA satellite. (NASA)

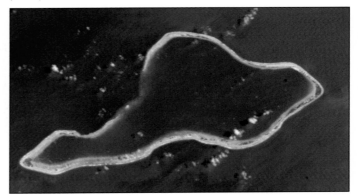

Muruoa (21° 50′ 00″ S, 138° 50′ 00″ W), seen from space in 2002. (NASA).

The fireball of *Dioné*, a test run on 5 June 1971. The device, under a balloon 275m above sea level, produced 34 kilotons. The *Dioné* explosion was monitored from a stand-off distance by a Victor of the British Royal Air Force based in Peru for the mission. (CEA)

Cordial intelligence

The CEP had the honour of receiving numerous overflights by Allied, American and British intelligence aircraft. The U-2 spy planes got the ball rolling in 1964. Operation *Fish Hawk* mobilized the aircraft carrier USS *Ranger*, carrying U-2s, which therefore had to be adapted for operations at sea as they were not designed for use at sea. Two U-2s were specially modified by Lockheed for landing

The equipment dedicated to the underground tests was directly derived from the oil and gas industry. (CEA)

This aerial picture of Mururoa in 1995 shows facilities, housing and the main road. Several logistic ships are visible in the small port used to support the tests. (Photo by Pierre Bayle)

landed, they were hidden in the hangar. Two flights were made, on 19 and 22 May, the missions involving taking photographs of what was going on at Tahiti, Mururoa and Hao.

On 12 June 1966, the French Navy spotted an unexpected visitor when the USS *Belmont*, a scientific vessel, entered inside the exclusion zone. On 1 July, a mysterious submarine was detected and a KC-135 Stratotanker was picked up by radar, obviously collecting atomic samples. On 9 July, the telemetry ship USS *Richfield* also violated the exclusion zone. Then on 12 July, another KC-135 was identified on the eve of the test. The CIA could thus confirm: the French would to go to the end of their ambition, thus preceding the missions of Operation *Burning Light* between 1966 and 1974 entrusted to specially modified C-135s.

The activities of the CEP also attracted the curiosity of the British, with the Royal Air Force mobilized. Between May and September 1971, the RAF command tasked two Handley Page Victors from 543 Squadron for a mission to survey what the French were up to at atolls some 5,800km from the coast of Peru. Sensors were specially adapted to measure radioactivity released by the explosions at the French atolls, while operating from international airspace. Integrated into the external tanks, these sensors were designed by scientists of the Atomic Weapons Research Establishment at Aldermarston. In order to approach the area, the aircraft were based at Lima airport in Peru. From there, they headed west for 1,000km to reach an area where they could collect atomic elements in the atmosphere. This was not the first such British operation. In 1969, the RAF had sent Camberra units and a Victor to monitor Chinese tests (Operations *Alchemist* and *Aroma*). For the 1971 missions, Operation *Attune* adopted an identical model. The British planes were tasked for three missions to monitor the tests code named *Dione* (5 June), Encélade (12 June) and Japet (4 July). The RAF missions were code named *Katina*, *Charlock* and *Lagonda*. When France put an end to its aerial tests, the Victors were re-tasked to monitor Chinese experiments.

These manoeuvres in the vicinity of the CEP did not lead to any official protest, the actions being seen, on the contrary, as a tribute, notably when French electronic systems intercepted the messages of the US crews after the explosions.

The technology challenge of underground tests

Underground tests had been introduced in 1975, on the decision of President Giscard d'Estaing, as they were safer for the environment and gave a larger and better collection of scientific data. A new technique based on experimental containers was developed. Large cylinders, about 20m long, were divided into three levels. At one end was the nuclear object, then the instruments for capturing the effects of the explosion and, at the other end, a transmission device connected to a fibre optic cable. Almost all of the space was occupied by electronic boxes. The container was then buried in a vertical

on the carrier, the plane receiving a reinforced train and a stock. The ship left San Francisco for its special mission, its air fleet seemingly limited to a few F-4 Phantoms in order to give the operation the appearance of a routine sortie. The vessel also carried special fuel for the U-2s. Piloted by Jim Barnes and Al Rand, a pair of the spy planes left Edwards AFB in California to join the ship at sea. As soon as they

The *Clemenceau* heading to the Pacific test range. To protect the first tests of the CEP, the French Navy gathered a significant force known as Force Alpha. On the flight deck are Étendard fighters and Alizé maritime patrol aircraft. The international impact of the tests was reinforced by this demonstration, which was also a message relating to the position of Paris within NATO. (*Marine Nationale*)

Commandant Henry, one of the escort ships detached for the protection of the Pacific test range. (*Marine Nationale*)

position at a great depth in the basalt bedrock. Everything then happened very quickly: the bomb exploded, the sensors collected the effects of the blast and the data was sent to the transmission module which sent everything to a control room for analysis by the CEA. According to witnesses, the vibrations felt on the surface evoked the passage of a metro underground train in Paris.

Jacques Chirac decided to end the moratorium on testing that had been signed off in 1991 by François Mitterrand, his socialist predecessor. The six last experiments were conducted in 1995 and 1996, to collect data to prepare the simulation programme. Their purpose was to provide the best scientific conditions before French adhesion to the comprehensive nuclear test ban treaty. This series ended with the *Xouthos* test. Two additional experiments were

scheduled, but considering the quality of the collected data, Chirac decided to stop the campaign. Thus, 27 January 1996 marked the last nuclear test in the history of France; two days later, the President announced the definitive end of French nuclear tests.

Mururoa and Fangataufa under the scrutiny of the United Nations: the environmental issue

The testing seriously affected the geology under the two atolls. The islands remain under the control of the French Army, which maintains units on them as the geological and radiological situation requires permanent monitoring, in a similar way that the US Department of Energy monitors the Nevada test site. Six aerial tests had generated large amounts of fallout: *Aldebaran* (2 July 1966, 28kt),

Vautours of the French Air Force were used to collect nuclear samples during the atmospheric tests directly in the atomic mushroom. *Escadron de Marche 85* was especially dedicated to the mission of collecting samples in the atmosphere. (Photo by Jean-Michel Guhl)

A '637 Missile' used to collect samples directly inside the atomic mushroom. This equipment had been developed by Matra and its sensors were designed by the CEA. (Collection Hervé Beaumont)

Arcturus (2 July 1967, 22kt), *Encelade* (12 June 1971, 440kt), *Phoebe* (8 August 1971, 4kt), *Centaure* (17 July 1974, 4kt) and perhaps *Rigel* (26 September 1966, 125kt). Airborne nuclear explosions in the Pacific have reached a total of 167 megatons, mostly carried out by the United States (including at Hiroshima and Nagasaki), the French

testing accounting for 11.8 megatons. In 1973, New Zealand, which was opposed to the French testing, sent the Leander-class frigate *Otago* to Mururoa in support of Greenpeace ships demonstrating against the tests. However, that same year, Australia, along with New Zealand, following the work of their scientific committees

A modular container for experimentation at Mururoa before an underground test. Close to the nuclear object was a chain of electronic sensors, with, at the aft section, transmission equipment. For these tests, French engineers developed unique very high-speed electronics. (B. Dumortier Collection)

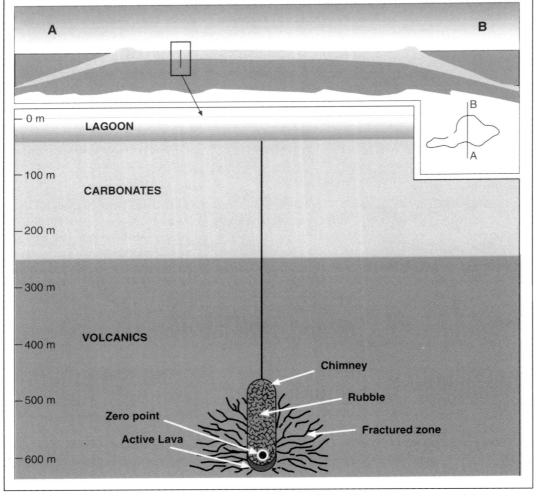

In 1972, it was decided to conduct exclusively underground tests. This had two advantages: a much better collection of data and a significant reduction in the effect on the environment. This chart gave details of arrangements for the underground tests, between 400 and 1,200m under the surface. (CEA)

on radiation, recognized that French aerial nuclear tests posed no danger to their populations.

Under the presidency of Jacques Chirac, a new orientation emerged in order to develop a controlled transparency on the nuclear tests in the Pacific Ocean. Times had changed. In the wake of the final testing campaign, the French government accepted a request by the International Atomic Energy Agency (IAEA) for a survey on the atolls under the direction of the United Nations. In order to analyse the effects of the experiments, the IAEA conducted a survey on Mururoa and Faugataufa between 26 May and 9 June 1997 to collect samples. It aimed to assess the situation in and around the atolls regarding the radiological and radiological effects of the tests on the local population. The mission was financed by French taxpayers and the IAEA and underlined the cooperative posture of French scientists. The IAEA reported that samples of underground water had been

Fangataufa, 27 January 1996: *Xouthos* was the 210th and final nuclear test in French military history. Xouthos was a Greek philosopher, a disciple of Pythagoras. In Greek mythology, he was the son of Helen and Orseis. Data collected thanks to the last test campaign of 1995–96 was sufficient to support the simulation programme. Consequently, Jacques Chirac decided to cancel the last two planned tests. Xouthos thus closed the chapter of the Cold War period as the French nuclear programme entered a new era. (CEA)

of people and which would be attributable to the estimated radiation doses that are now being received or that would be received in the future by people as a result of the residual radioactive material at Mururoa and Fangataufa Atolls." The report also emphasized that with the very low levels estimated in the survey, there would be no changes in cancer rates in the region attributable to radiation caused by the residual radioactive material at the atolls. The IAEA continued: "The Study concluded that no further environmental monitoring at Mururoa and Fangataufa Atolls is needed for purposes of radiological protection."

From an operational point of view, the tests took advantage of the latest updates

collected from two tests cavities beneath Mururoa and from deep in the carbonate layer beneath the lagoons. The results provided an independent validity of radionuclide concentrations in the cavity-chimney of each test.

The IAEA insisted: "The French Government allowed complete access to the atolls for these surveys and provided the necessary logistic support." The report stated: "The Study concluded that there will be no radiation health effects which could be either medically diagnosed in an individual or epidemiologically discerned in a group

in electronic technologies and data-processing of the 1970s, 1980s and 1990s, giving French scientists a very high level of know-how in the domain of nuclear explosions, a strong legacy to shift their nuclear researches into the simulation programme of the post-Cold War period. Three technologies were explored in three separate laboratories: high-power laser, high-power computing and radiography. It is a story that will have to be told in the second volume of this series.

7
HOOKED ATOMS: COOPERATION WITH HISTORIC PARTNERS

For Paris, the choice for nuclear cooperation was reduced to a few nations. The Americans were contacted, Paris exploiting all the ways offered by NATO, while cultivating the spirit of the Battle of Yorktown. There was also contact with Israel in a complicity and intimacy unprecedented in the history of international relations. The talks with the US were part of a long-term approach that continues today, whereas with Israel, the honeymoon ended in divorce. Nuclear cooperation with the United Kingdom was much reduced, with just an intervention with the thermonuclear formula, as seen in a previous chapter. The Franco-British axis was instead expressed elsewhere: Concorde and the Jaguar tactical aircraft. A structural obstacle was that military nuclear weaponsand their doctrine was evolving at the highest levels, so even between allies, cooperation was complicated. Yet France managed this process to find its own way, with success, considering a close view of its sovereignty. When the CEA was founded in October 1945, French atomists who had fled to Canada in 1940 after the defeat by Germany returned to launch the new nuclear era.

Officials in Washington wonder "should we support or counter French ambitions?"

In the beginning, the nation had to rely for the nuclear project on its own resources. With the USA, it would be a relationship built step-by-step, according to the interests of the moment. The US intelligence community placed French ambitions under scrutiny. It was public knowledge that the atom bomb was a French ambition. In a letter to President Roosevelt, Albert Einstein mentioned Frédéric Joliot-Curie in the field of nuclear research. However, things went wrong from the start, due notably to the hostility of General Leslie Grove, the director of the Manhattan Project (development of the US atom bomb), towards French scientists. The French team was not allowed to join the research being carried out at Los Alamos. Hans Alban and Lew Kowaski, the two deputies of Joliot, who quit occupied France in June 1940, would have to continue their work in Canada, where they had taken refuge. The 'bomb' would be developed without them. There was, however, some success: among the 'free nuclear French', Bertrand Golschmitt found a way to extract plutonium from irradiated uranium bars. But mistrust was such that General Groove came to imagine the kidnapping of Joliot during

A B-58 Hustler of the US Air Force. As the features of the American aircraft were close to those of the Mirage IV, French officers were allowed to go to Omaha in Nebraska and Caswell in Texas to attend the standard training programme arranged for the airmen of the US Strategic Air Command. (US Air Force)

The Boeing KC-135 was the most visible symbol of the support of the US administration to the French strategy of deterrence. Between March 1963 and January 1964, nine crews selected to serve in the Tankers underwent conversion on the aircraft at Lackland and Castle air force bases. Renamed C-135FR (for France), the Boeings of the FAS integrated a national radio-communication system and a refuelling device similar to those of the US Navy to connect with the probe of the Mirage IV. (*Forces aériennes stratégiques*)

the United Kingdom. Peace being restored in Europe made it possible to hope for some minimal aid according to the adage 'Help yourself, America will help you'. The communists were excluded from the French *IVe Republique*, which was definitely in the Atlantic camp. As a founding member of NATO, France benefitted both from the Marshall Plan to restore the economy and from offshore orders to rebuild its defence industry. American funding thus supported the production of the Ouragan fighter at the Dassault factories. However, there were no nuclear links between Paris and Washington. First, there was the cancellation at the last moment of Operation *Vultur* in 1954, a nuclear raid by the US Air Force to loosen the grip of Vietminh troops encircling the French at Dien Bien Phu.

the liberation of Paris in August 1944. To make matters worse, the scientist did not mask his own communist sympathies.

Then came the atom bombs dropped at Hiroshima and Nagasaki in August 1945. Washington, logically, wanted to maintain its nuclear monopoly, hence the McMahon Act which aimed to block any transfer of nuclear knowledge to any foreign nation, including

Then came the humiliation of Suez in 1956. On balance, France was seen, internationally, to be in retreat, in the Far East and the Levant. Socialists and Gaullists understood this: the atom bomb was sovereign, so the project became a military one.

France remained a full member of NATO even after its departure from the planning commitee in 1966, still respecting the collective defence principles written into Article 5 of the treaty. Under the mandate of Valéry Giscard d'Estaing (1974–81), the diplomatic atmosphere was much better with Washington, with coordination procedures set up between the respective chiefs of staff on nuclear strike scenarios. (NATO)

French driving: to cut in turns

The atomic ambition was a race against time. The Cold War context argued in favour of Paris. Between official exchanges and 'information' gleaned here or there, through encounters and scientific readings, the French learned a lot about their American friends. Enough to cut certain things, to choose the good options, saving time and money. Colonel Charles Ailleret spent two weeks in Las Vegas to attend a nuclear test in Nevada. Devoting himself to 'special' weapons, he would be in charge of building the French test range in the desert of Algeria. The Americans let themselves be convinced by the French, which led to a minimal agreement signed on 7 May 1959 clearing the delivery of enriched uranium for a prototype reactor on land, the mandatory technical milestone to prepare the future nuclear submarines. This was based on a Westinghouse design, which was also communicated to the French. This agreement saved the ambition of France to build its own fleet of nuclear submarines after the total failure of the Q244 project.

Meanwhile, the first Mirage IV crews trained in a B-58 unit, the American plane being close to the Dassault Delta, and followed the same course as their colleagues from the US Air Force. As Eastern Europe was a surface-to-air missile trap for enemy aircraft, French Air Force delegations visited Wright Patterson in Dayton, Ohio, to learn about self-protection measures for the Mirage IV. The SA-2 missile useages in Vietnam provided good examples. Navigation equipment was purchased in the US for the Dassault bomber and licenses were acquired from Kerfot. At Sagem, navigation technology experts, know-how was reinforced thanks to their civil

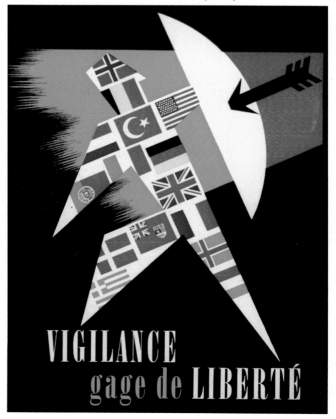

A NATO educational brochure from 1960. (NATO)

The Hawk air-defence missile system, a US-made product sold to France to equip the French Army. (NATO)

Launch of an Honest John missile during a drill of an artillery regiment of the French Army. Along with F-100 Super Sabre squadrons, the French forces were tasked to deliver US tactical nuclear bombs within the defence strategy of the Atlantic Alliance. (NATO)

proposal made in Paris to provide Atlas missiles to deliver the French warheads.

Shopping trip in the USA

The French Army received Hawk anti-aircraft missiles. French chemists jumped at this chance to analyse its booster, for the benefit of strategic engines. US exports supported the ambitions of the French armed forces. In 1963, for the *Clemenceau* and the *Foch*, the navy was able to acquire 42 Crusader interceptors, as well as anti-aircraft missiles for the escort ships. The French Navy conducted anti-submarine missions with a fleet of P-2 Neptunes, V-6 upgraded versions being commissioned in 1958 in contracts equivalent to those in Canada, the United Kingdom, Netherlands,

programmes, its workshops being in charge of the maintenance of the inertial platforms of the Boeing 707 operated by Air France, the national carrier being the first international customer of Boeing's airliner. A small group of officers was welcomed at the US Strategic Air Command to visit ICBM sites. One conclusion was clear: solid propulsion was preferable to hazardous liquid fuel engines. Nevertheless, President de Gaulle finally rejected the American

Portugal, Argentina, Australia, Brazil and Japan. The French Army, in the early 1960s, learned a lot about the use of the weapon in its F-100 Super Saber and Honest John surface-to-surface rocket units. Then came 'the' big issue: in-flight refuelling. Paris issued a request to purchase Boeing C-135 Stratotankers for the Strategic Air Forces; President Kennedy rejected the anti-France lobby in the USA and a contract was signed in July 1962. The FAS was to receive 12 'FR' variant C-135s to refuel the Mirage IV. The commander of the US Air

A meeting of David Ben Gourion (left), Prime Minister of Israel, and Charles de Gaulle at the Elysée Palace on 13 June 1960. Both characters shared the same sense of tragedy in history – but their military backgrounds were fundamentally different. (Government of Israel)

Force, General Curtis LeMay, was said to have declared: "Since they have Mirage IVs, let us help them to use them as well as possible." Failing that, Paris had a plan B: to transform the Caravelle. Kennedy's gesture of support can be considered as an implicit recognition of the French nuclear force, but Robert McNamara, his Secretary of Defense, was opposed to the development of independent nuclear forces within NATO. In the operational sphere, cooperation remained excellent and contracts were signed for France to buy heavy cargo planes, the C-141 Starlifter or C-5 Galaxy. However, following the oil crisis, for budgetary reasons, the French airmen would never be cleared to buy the transport aircraft of their dreams.

One field remained excluded for France: the design of the nuclear payloads. However, electronic warfare was open to a certain level of cooperation. French airmen would always be very involved in NATO's EW campaigns: Mace (electromagnetic) and Embow (infra-red). Discipline was critical. When Dassault studied a Super Mirage IV, US aerospace manufacturer Pratt & Whitney was allowed to supply the engines and signed a license with Snecma. Meanwhile, the French CT-41 ramjet target drone had seduced the US Navy, with six acquired by Bell Aircraft for evaluation by the navy, which used the supersonic missile at Point Mugu. Bell also acquired a license for this missile, which in 1962 received the US designation PQM-56A. In the engine domain, Snecma signed a strategic cooperation in civil engines with General Electric in 1974 that led to the CFM International consortium. An agreement between President Richard Nixon and his opposite number, Georges Pompidou, speeded up the process. CFM thereafter became the world's leading supplier of commercial aircraft engines, delivering to date (the early 2020s) more than 37,500 engines to more than 570 operators. As of 2022, the US-French joint venture holds 40 percent of the world's commercial aircraft engine market share.

Thomas Reed and Danny Stilman explored this partnership in a book, *Nuclear Express*, detailing an agreement signed in 1973 between French Defence Minister Robert Galley and his US counterpart, James Schlesinger, authorising French engineers to test equipment during nuclear experiments in Nevada. The historian of the French strike force, Jacques Villain, summed up the situation as follows: "Thanks to American freedom of information and the benevolence, voluntary or not, of the American administration, the French taxpayer's money has been saved."

A strategic alliance with Israel

On atomic affairs, the CEA did not have many partners to turn to in the 1950s. The Americans did not want to give away their secrets, under the McMahon Act. As for their British allies, they were linked to the agreements signed with Washington. Germany or Italy were, of course, still impossible at this time. How the French ended up liaising with Israeli scientists is outlined in the book *The President and the Bomb*, by Jean Guisnel (a historian and journalist who

Inside the MD620 Dassault factory near Bordeaux. Teams of Israeli engineers and technicians went to France to learn about the manufacturing processes of the missile. (Dassault Aviation)

A test of the MD-620 tactical ballistic missile at Ile du Levant, off the French Riviera. Dassault was awarded the development of the missile for Israel with the official support of the government. (Dassault Aviation)

was expert in defence matters) and Bruno Tertrais (a member of the Parisian think tank *Fondation pour la Recherche Strategique)*. In their book, they state that a strategic alliance with Tel Aviv made sense. Paris shared the same hostility as Israel towards Nasser, the Egyptian leader who helped the FLN national movement in Algeria in a war against the Fourth Republic. Backed by the sea, in a tricky strategic position, Israel needed an ally in the face of the hostility of its neighbours. Jacques Soustelle had an important role at the highest level of the French administration in 1959, being appointed Minister Delegate (*de facto* Deputy Prime Minister) to Prime Minister

A Jericho launcher just after lift-off from the Palmachin range, south-west of Tel-Aviv. The Israeli ballistic missile was a direct evolution of the French technology developed by Dassault for Israel. (IAI)

Michel Debré. In this position, Soustelle was in charge of nuclear affairs, and he worked hard to develop relations with Israel. A Gaullist from the start (he joined *France Libre* in July 1940), he was also the president of the France-Israel Alliance, an association he founded in 1956. The foundations of this cooperation were laid from 17–19 June 1956 at the Château de Vemars in the suburbs of Paris. Around the table were Abel Thomas, Chief of Staff to Maurice Bourguès-Maunoury, the French Minister of Defence; Pierre Boursicot, head of the French secret service; General

A Lockheed U-2 on the USS *America* prepares for an intelligence mission over the nuclear test range in French Polynesia. The mission was eventually flown from the USS *Ranger*. (US DoD)

An RAF Victor during Operation *Attune*, an intelligence campaign by the United Kingdom regarding the atmospheric nuclear tests conducted in the Pacific. (RAF)

A heavily modified RC-135 intelligence aircraft of the *Burning Light* mission. The aircraft were based in Hawaii and then headed to French Polynesia to collect radioactive elements just after an atmospheric test. (US DoD)

Maurice Challe, Chief of the Defence Staff; and the Israelis Moshe Dayan, Shimon Peres and Yehoshafat Harkabi, of Israel's military intelligence. Once the groundwork had been done, Guy Mollet, President of the Council, and Defence Minister Bourguès-Maunoury were in Sèvres on 22 July to welcome their Israeli counterparts.

During talks in this charming suburban town to the west of Paris, which was chosen for its discretion, Mollet and Bourguès-Maunoury agreed to build a nuclear power plant in Israel. The agreement was so secret that nothing was consigned to paper, but the summit of Sèvres is now part of the shared history of the two nations. Shimon Peres later signed a contract with Saint-Gobain in October 1957 for the plant to be located at Dimona in southern Israel. The CEA, under the direction of Pierre Guillaumat, was part of the project. Located in the heart of the Negev desert, it was

intended that the plant would not attract curiosity, it being officially designated a textile factory. However, designed on the same model as the Marcoule nuclear power plant in France, Dimona was built to be able to produce plutonium.

The work was carried out under the auspices of companies specially chosen by the CEA whose names could not give any hint of the reality of their profession. The construction was entrusted to the *Societé Alsacienne de Construction Mécanique* (SACM), which later became the Financing and Business Study Company (SEFE). The reactor was entrusted to the *Société Industrielle d'Etude et de Construction Chimique*, a nominee of Saint-Gobain. More than 300 French people were working on site in the Negev desert. Many of them moved to Israel with their families, which provided a Gallic hint to the city of Beer-Sheva, 13km to the east of the site. French could

The CT-41 supersonic target drone. The missile was purchased by the US Navy and used at Point Mugu naval base. French advances in ramjet technology was of great interest to the Pentagon, which also financed research flights with the Griffon experimental aircraft. (Aerospatiale)

General Charles 'Chuck' Yaeger, the famous American test pilot, visited the Mirage IVA production line at Dassault Factory in the 1960s. Saved by the Resistance during the war, Yaeger had a special relationship with the French. (Dassault Aviation)

be heard spoken in the city's streets, while local restaurants adapted menus from Paris and provided traditional French cooking. Such details aroused the suspicions of the CIA, which directed U-2 spy planes to fly over the area to discover just what was going on. Years later, in 1986, Mordechaï Vanunu, an engineer from Dimona, caused irreparable damage to the project, providing the *Sunday Times* in London with pictures revealing the installations at the site. Subsequently captured by Israeli agents, Vanunu was sentenced to 18 years in prison. He was released on probation in 2004, with a ban on him meeting journalists.

As work on the Dimona site was being carried out, General de Gaulle reassured Israel about France's commitment to the project. The strategic relationship between the countries was accompanied by the delivery of French arms: first Ouragan fighters, Mystères, then Mirage IIIs and above all MD-620 missiles, a

Richard Nixon and Georges Pompidou met for talks at Reykjavik in 1973. Thanks to the political support of the two leaders, General Electric and Snecma inked an agreement on the development of a new commercial engine, the CFM-56. The engine would equip several military versions of the Boeing KC-135. In the wake of an agreement between the respective ministries of defence, French engineers were able to test devices during nuclear tests in Nevada. (National Archives)

An American Pershing II missile. François Mitterrand warmly supported NATO deploying cruise missiles and Pershing IIs in Europe in order to balance the new Soviet SS-20 missiles. "The pacifists are in the West, and the missiles are in the East," he declared on 20 January 1983 at the Bundestag of Federal Germany. The pacifist movements remained weak in France in comparison with their massive support in Germany and Great Britain. One possible explanation may be the confidence of the French in their home-grown nuclear force and the efficiency of deterrence. (NATO)

strategic weapon specifically manufactured by Dassault for Israel. Matters then began to turn sour. Just after the Six-Day War, President de Gaulle decreed an arms embargo, an opportunity for France to restore Arab diplomacy. The Mirage V ordered by Israel was not delivered, instead being donated to the French Air Force. Valéry Giscard d'Estaing maintained terrible relations with Israel in the 1970s. In reaction, the Israelis turned to the US and built a home defence industry that is today one of the most efficient in the world, notably in electronics and later in drones. France then quickly gave Israel the instruments of autonomy. However, Franco-Israeli relations suffer greatly when France delivered a nuclear complex to Iraqi leader Saddam Hussein. In response, on 7 June 1981, Israeli Prime Minister Menachem Begin approved the launch of Operation *Opera*, during which F-15s and F-16s from Heyl Ha'Avir head for Al-Tuwaitha south of Baghdad and destroyed the Osirak reactor in a daring raid. France had to wait for the presidency of Nicolas Sarkozy in the early 2000s for an official warming of relations with Israel. Meanwhile, the world had changed, and Israel signed a peace agreement with Jordan. Alain Juppé, several times Minister of Foreign Affairs and then Prime Minister under Jacques Chirac in 1986, precisely outlined the importance of Israel to France: "For us the security of Israel is sacred." He was speaking in 2018 in the rooms of Quai d'Orsay, at the heart of French diplomacy, in a TV programme on the Parliamentary Channel.

Finding a balance between interdependence and sovereignty

French deterrence differs from the choice of London, which has consolidated its transatlantic cooperation with the application of treaties: Quebec (1943), Bermuda (1957) and Nassau (1962). Taking advantage of American Polaris, Poseidon and then Trident missiles, the British nuclear force remains integrated within NATO inside the Nuclear Planning Group. General de Gaulle, and all his successors, took advantage of France's favourable geographical position in Europe. France was located as the second line of defence, Germany forming the front line against the forces of the Warsaw Pact. This scheme is still relevant in the 2020s with regard to the allies of Eastern Europe which are now members of NATO. In a consecrated nuclear alliance, NATO places the French strike force on a par with the Americans and the British, a principle laid down by the official Ottawa declaration of 1973 and since never denied.

8
PHANTOM FORCE

When France decided on the composition of its strike force through the 1960–1964 military acquisition law, Washington had already formatted a strategic standard: submarines armed with ballistic missiles, intercontinental missiles and long-range bombers. The strategic architecture was already fixed. However, there was a phantom French nuclear force. Presidential choices were, and are, a function of a perception of the facts: the principle of sufficiency and the balance of power in the Atomic age. In the 1950s and 1960s, all technological directions were still open to the carrying of the nuclear bomb. Due to uncertain concepts and budgetary challenges, the choices would ultimately fall on the most immediately accessible technologies. French resources were limited, and politicians – especially de Gaulle – wanted to move quickly. It is worth noting that this enthusiasm for high-risk projects was not specifically French.

Fantastical missiles
While the future of a ballistic missiles force was still uncertain, projects for long-range atmospheric weapons were multiplying. These projects often reused the solution tested on ramjet aircraft by engineer René Leduc. At the beginning of the 1950s, there were the designs of the SE-X-223 and SE-X223 of the SNCASE (*Société nationale des constructions aéronautiques du Sud-Est*) arsenal. With futuristic lines, these 'robots' with gleaming aluminium fuselages and their delta wings would not have looked out of in a Jerry Anderson TV series. The rockets quickly competed with the air-breathing missiles. Their shape was close to the SE-212 Durandal, a prototype of a combat aircraft that flew for the first time in 1956 and featured an innovative propulsion system composed of a standard reactor and a ramjet. However, the French airmen ultimately preferred the

Mirage for its better performances and potential evolutions. The Redstone tactical rocket (1953) and the launch of Sputnik (1957) cleared the path for the carrying of the 'bomb'. At the end of the 1950s, a first French ballistic project was launched: the SSBT, or tactical ballistic ground-to-ground missile. The project was a part of the diplomacy of the *IVe Republique*. Named *Casseur* ('striker'), this weapon would give Paris a more visible position within NATO itself, at a time when Germany has just been authorized to rebuild its armed forces. The SSBT was examined by the Committee of Chiefs of Staff in May 1957. An 8.5m missile on a truck, the *Casseur* had a maximum range of 100km. This tactical weapon met the challenges of solid propulsion and inertial navigation, two domains that French engineers had to master.

Charles de Gaulle, who returned to power in May 1958, wanted more ambitious projects. Officials then studied the air-surface ballistic strategic missile project. Matra was quick out of the starting blocks with the Matra 600. Once released from a plane, the missile could rapidly descend under radar coverage. Powered by a turbojet engine, this heavy missile had a range of 2,400km. The carrier was a modified Breguet Atlantic tasked with ensuring a permanent aerial alert with its weapons. For this purpose, an in-flight refuelling probe was integrated. The internal capability was extended by removing the maritime radar and the magnetic detector. The concept of in-flight alerts, on the other hand, required a high operating budget, but above all carried an unacceptable risk of accidents. The concept of nuclear aircraft on patrol gave way to land-based supersonic aircraft on alert, ready for take-off on very short notice, without taking into account the vulnerability of a plane flying at 540km/h. From a political point of view, it would have been difficult to imagine

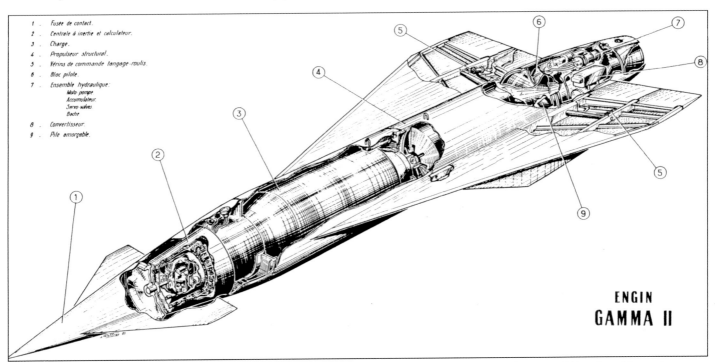

Dassault's proposed the Gamma II project was a delta wing missile that would offer a standoff capability to the Mirage IV bombers. The nuclear payload was located at the centre of the fuselage. The weapon weighed over 4,500lb, had a range of 300km and a top speed of Mach 3. (Hervé Beaumont Collection)

ENGIN "GAMMA IV"

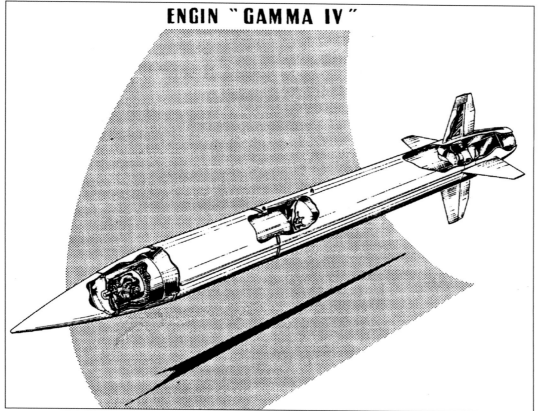

Gamma IV was a project for an air-to-ground missile with a range of 400km. Part of the Minerve project, it was a heavy missile with a weight of 3.3 tons. It was mainly imagined to equip an extended version of the Mirage IV. (Hervé Beaumont Collection)

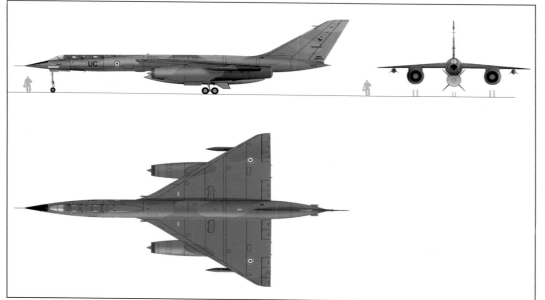

A project of heavy supersonic bombers was proposed by the Minerve project. It was planned to equip the aircraft with a specific supersonic air-to ground missile. (Fana de l'Aviation)

could strike at a distance of 10,000km in order to extend deterrence towards China, which had just demonstrated its thermonuclear capability. It corresponded to the all-azimuth deterrence strategy desired by de Gaulle. Measuring 25m long, the SSLP was even bigger than the LGM-30 Minuteman. However, it was cancelled in 1969 as it was too expensive. It would have required new re-entry vehicles considering the level of thermal and mechanical effects, but also a new inertial guidance to obtain the required precision. The S-2 and then S-3 missiles in silos were considered sufficient to deter the immediate threat from the East. Technically risky, the SSLP would have greatly exceeded the objectives assigned to French nuclear strategy.

Verdun: a longer aircraft carrier

In 1949, the French Navy had the ambition to construct four large aircraft carriers, a figure quickly reduced to three. The *IVe Republique* then launched the PA54 *Clemenceau*. Laid down in November 1955, it was followed by the PA55 *Foch*, its building beginning in February 1957. A third was expected to replace the *Arromanches*, which was scheduled to be decommissioned in 1962. The French Navy saw its future on a grand scale, and this resulted in the motivation for the PA58 project, which was expected in the 1958 fiscal year. The limits of the aviation on board the Clemenceau class – Étendard IV light fighters – resulted in the argument for the *Verdun*

a consensus in the population for a permanent programme with nuclear weapons in the sky. US Air Force B-52 accidents, with their B-58 H-bombs on board, at Palomares in Spain (17 January 1966) and Thule in Greenland (21 January 1968) proved the weakness of the operational scheme. In addition, the Sud-Aviation supersonic missile derived from the 2,500km-range X-422 did not convince the French. Paris thus complied with Washington's cancellation of an equivalent, the Skybolt, designed in the United Kingdom. In 1967, another project was discarded: the SSLP or *Sol-Sol Longue Portée* (Ground-ground Long Range) missile. This heavy ICBM

project. A tribute to the crucial battle of 1916, this ship would never see the light of day. It was to have been calibrated to accommodate a naval version of the Mirage IVA. Externally, the *Verdun* was an extension of the Clemenceau class. The displacement was increased to 45,000 tons at full load and the flight deck extended over 286m so as to integrate 100m catapults. Its self-defence armament was luxurious: 100mm turrets, two Masurca long-range surface-to-air systems with 60 missiles in reserve, a towed sonar and two Malafon torpedo missile ramps. Its 200,000 cv (the French equivalent of hp) of propulsion would have given the vessel a top speed of 35 knots,

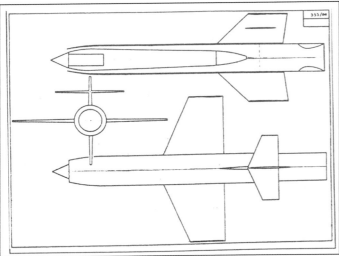

A project for a strategic cruise missile boosted by ramjet engines would have had a range of over 5,000km. This project, similar in concept to the American Snark missile, would get no further than the drawing board. (Document Aerospatiale/Airbus)

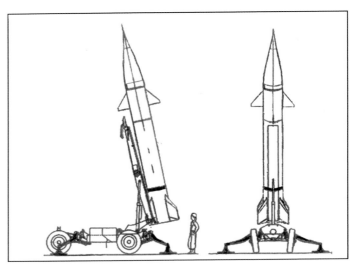

The Casseur (or Striker) was a project for a tactical nuclear missile considered by the *IVe Republique* at the end of the 1950s. This short-range ground-to-ground project was dismissed by Charles de Gaulle in favour of more ambitious systems. (Aerospatiale/Airbus).

The Balzac VTOL project featured an elegant airframe and a supersonic speed that achieved its first stationary flight on 12 October 1962. The aircraft marked the start of modern electrical flight controls and was the first to transmit flight data to the ground by telemetry. (Dassault Aviation)

Developed by Dassault Aviation, the Mirage 4000 project was a heavy multi-role aircraft developed in the l1970s to replace the Mirage IV. For the designer, it was the logic continuation of the Mirage IV for the strategic mission. The Mirage 4000 featured over 6 tons of external payloads, two M-53 engines plus a long-range radar. (Dassault Aviation)

An artist's impression of the Super Mirage 4000 equipped with the ASMP nuclear missile and the colours of the French Air Force. The Rafale, armed with the ASMP-A missile, can be regarded as the culmination of this concept. (*Fana de l'Aviation*)

Project ACT 92 (*Avion de combat tactique*) unveiled at the end of the 1970s by Dassault Aviation had foreshadowed the future architecture that paved the way for the Rafale. (Dassault Aviation)

had in its roadmap: the new ASMP and its launch platform, the Super Étendard, which had a refuelling probe. Later on, deterrence in form of an aircraft carrier became the mission of the *Charles-de-Gaulle*, the Rafale fighter-bomber and the ASMP-A missile, which had a range of several thousand kilometres.

Why not a Super Mirage IV?

In 1957, when the Mirage IVA programme had been launched for a year, officials at Dassault imagined an extrapolation, the Mirage IVB. The idea was to compensate for the deemed insufficient range of the IVA to strike in the East. The length of the new version was to be increased to 27.8m, compared to 23.5m for the Mirage IVA. The wing surface, 130m², was doubled. Speed would increases to Mach 2.3 and its range would reaches 4,400km without refuelling. On 18 March 1959, three prototypes were ordered. Pratt & Whitney received an order for 10 engines, the J-75 B-24, that Snecma would manufacture under license. However, the C-135FR tankers purchased from Boeing made the Mirage IVB over-specified; the contracts were cancelled. Thereafter, Nord Aviation, the historic

double that of the American carrier USS *Enterprise*. However, the French Navy came to realise that it could already guarantee the permanence at sea of its carrier battle groups with its current modern aircraft carriers, while the bulk of its deterrence was achieved with its ballistic missile submarines. The *Verdun*, 30 percent more expensive than the Clemenceau class (excluding aviation), was definitively abandoned in 1971, just before the entry into service of the first sub of the Redoutable class. Rationally, given the costs, the French aircraft carriers were now to focus on conventional actions, although reserving the option of arming them with AN52 tactical bombs was decided upon in the 1970s. The French Navy

A mock-up of the ASLP project displayed at the Paris Air Show at the booth of Aerospatiale in 1991. The first works were budgeted by the DGA, the French armament directorate. With a range of over 1,000km and a stealth design, the ASLP (*Air-sol-longue-portée*) missile was proposed to the British at the end of the 1980s within a new cooperation in nuclear affairs. The ASLP was seen as a replacement for the ASMP. It was displayed close to a mock-up of the ASMP, a message of continuation between the two weapons. (Photo by author)

competitor of Marcel Dassault, proposed in 1962 a large delta propelled by two engines in nacelles, a sort of 'tricolor B-58 Hustler'.

Piloted by a crew of three seated in tandem, the Minerve bomber was an elegant aircraft of 58 tons, having a length of 34m and a wingspan of 19.5m. Its armament was an 8-ton missile. Hopes for a 'super bomber' reappeared in the 1970s at Dassault with the Balzac and then the Mirage 4000. With two M-53 engines, the aircraft was twice as powerful as the Mirage 2000. The '4000' would be Dassault's last manned prototype and very nearly went into production. The supersonic twin-engine aircraft was launched in September 1976. Its performance was exceptional: a payload capacity of 8 tons, a long-range radar and unprecedented manoeuvrability thanks to electric flight controls and a mobile canard configuration. Jacques Chirac proposed in 1981 that if elected as President of France, he would provide the air force with around 100 Mirage 4000s to replace the fleet of already aging Mirage IV. However, the economic slowdown then imposed a painful review of ambitions, and the Mirage 2000 would instead be the standard French combat aircraft from 1984. The Mirage 4000 would, however, be used for the development of the Rafale project, and thus carried out nearly 290 test flights in that role. The Dassault Balzac, a vertical take-off and landing (VTOL) testbed of the early 1960s, also has its place in the gallery of proposed French types. For VTOL sequences, the aircraft integrated eight Rolls-Royce RB108 lift engines. The project came about after a request by the French Air Force for a new recce and tactical strike aircraft. After an accident involving the prototype on 10 January 1964 during its 125th sortie, then a fatal crash of the second prototype on 8 September 1965, officials decided to stop the programme in 1965. On the positive side, the Balzac configuration was so innovative that

Dassault had achieved progress in electric flight controls on a Mach 2 airframe.

One parameter that also came into the game was the strength of Soviet air-defence missiles, as had been witnessed by the American air forces in Vietnam, which shifted the situation regarding raids at medium and high altitude. The credibility of nuclear deterrence required efforts in electronic warfare, an area which had a great future; critical and spectacular in its effects, it saved the notion of air power. The principle of technological and operational sufficiency of the French nuclear strategy imposed limits on the specifications of what was strictly necessary. This explains the cancellation in 1993 of the Franco-British ASLP (Air-Sol-Long Range) missile, a stealth weapon that could strike beyond 1,000 km, as a successor to the ASMP. The credibility of the nuclear force meant an avoidance of any risks inherent in projects that were deemed too fanciful.

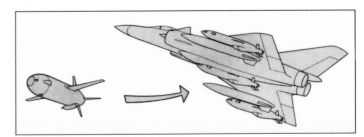

Proposed at the end of the 1970s, this is a heavy configuration of the Mirage 4000 fighter-bomber loaded with three cruise missiles. Actually, the programme for such missiles had to be postponed, due to a lack of space imagery and modelling terrain software. (Document Dassault Aviation).

9

NUCLEAR TOURISM IN FRANCE

Already a touristic superpower thanks to its many castles and historic cities, France has a large number of museums dedicated to its nuclear works. The spirit of these permanent exhibitions express themselves in a positive environment, French public opinion being widely in favour of the nuclear strategy. These museums are also an expression of the national pride around the strategic triad and the technological achievements in the nuclear field. Open to the public, these places are part of an educative voyage within France.

Paris – The Radium Institute

Close to Le Pantheon, in the Latin district of Paris, the Radium Institute is the place where Marie Curie conducted her works in chemistry. In Parisian-style architecture, its construction began in 1911. Surrounded by trees and a small romantic garden, the museum presents scientific instruments, photographs, documents and texts on the history of radioactivity and its medical applications, as well as panels on the life and work of 'the family of five Nobel prizes'. Many scientific instruments used until the end of the 1930s are on display, in particular those used to detect radioelements. In these rooms, in January 1934, Frédéric and Irène Joliot-Curie discovered artificial radioactivity. The visitor can walk through Marie Curie's

old office, as well as her chemistry laboratory, but there is no need to worry about radioactivity as the place was decontaminated in 1981. In 2012, the museum was renovated and now offers several themes: the Curie family and the Nobel prizes; radium, its features and applications; the Curie laboratory; and the Curie Foundation to fight cancer. The message also has a political side concerning the position of Frédéric Joliot-Curie in the military dimension of nuclear science.

Le Bourget, Air and Space Museum

Located just 10km north of Paris, the *Musée de l'air et de l'Espace* at Le Bourget is a must-see for anyone with an interest in the history of aviation and space. The museum naturally focuses on France's ambitions in this fileld. Among the civil aircraft covering two centuries of flight, several rooms concentrate on the development of nuclear weapons, missiles and bombers. Le Bourget was the place where Charles Lindbergh landed after achieving the first flight over the Atlantic. The curator is under the authority of the Ministry of Defence. Much of what can now be seen there is due to General Jean-Paul Siffre, a former Mirage IV pilot who in the 1990s carried out ambitious work to improve the visibility of strategic weapons

The Radium Institute features exhibits and artefacts of the Curie dynasty. The nuclear adventure of France was born here, in this laboratory. Close to the Pantheon, in the *5e arrondissement* of Paris, this museum is part of the Curie Institute, a research centre working against cancers. (Photo by author)

The Air and Space Museum at Le Bourget. In the room devoted to the space programme are a S-3 ground-to-ground missile and a series of ballistic missiles of the first two decades of French nuclear deterrence. One of the underground command posts of the missiles polygon of *Plateau d'Albion* has also been recreated, along with sounding rockets and special sub-systems. (Photo by author)

The *Musée de l'air et de l'Espace* at Le Bourget includes exhibits of French combat aviation in the 1950s and 1960s and examples of the fierce competition between state-owned corporates and Marcel Dassault: the Mystère IV, Mirage III, Balzac, an experimental VTOL aircraft and two prototypes, the SO 9000 Trident rocket aircraft (*Société nationale des constructions aéronautiques du Sud-Ouest*) and Griffon (Nord Aviation). (Photo by author)

and space activities. The assortment of military systems on display including a series of ground-to-ground missiles, the first generation of sea-based ballistic missiles and testbed re-entry vehicles. Among the relics gathered, visitors can see one of the first inertial navigation units, a re-entry vehicle, the underground command post of *Plateau d'Albion* and the cap of the Ariane booster which placed into orbit Helios, the first military imagery satellite that was launched in December 1995.

All objects are remarkably well preserved. Indoors, the prototypes room underlines the efforts in the 1950s of the aeronautic industry to find the best solutions that opened the path to supersonic flight with the Mirage IV and Concorde commercial liner.

Inside the collection of the European Aviation Museum in Montélimar is a Mirage IV A in its aluminium overall livery. The bomber is part of a collection of 70 combat aircraft, most in an excellent state of preservation. Mirage IV no.28, a prototype of the 'IVP' upgraded version is displayed at the Clément Ader Museum in Lyon. (Photo by author)

At The City of the Sea in Cherbourg in Normandy, *Le Redoutable* is the only nuclear strategic submarine in the world to have been transformed into a museum. (Photo by author)

La Cité de la Mer, Cherbourg

In the port town of Cherbourg in Normandy, The City of the Sea (*La Cité de la Mer*) includes an opportunity to visit *Le Redoutable*, the only strategic ballistic nuclear submarine in the world that has been transformed into a museum for the public. Visitors enter the giant *Le Redoutable* through a small door in the aft section of the hull. You will first enter the propulsion room, and can then discover the forest of tubes in the engine room and reactor control room, the missiles section – with its 16 vertical tubes – the operation and navigation centre, crew and officers' cabins, the canteen and the torpedo room with its former munitions. The nuclear reactor has been removed to obtain clearance for public visits. The working bakery close to the kitchen produces fresh baguettes every day and croissants on Sunday. *La Cité de la Mer* encompasses many aspects of maritime activities: biology, the environment, literature around a Jules Verne theme, exploration of the oceans, deep-sea diving and of course scientific and military submarines. Officially opened on 30 July 1933, the passenger terminal was an amazing achievement of the Art Deco era. Designed by the architect Levavasseur, the station became the largest liner terminal in the world and the second most extensive building in France after the Palace of Versailles. *La Cité de la Mer* was opened on 29 April 2002, its main attractions being *Le Redoutable* and a room of simulators for children. It has since had over 4 million visitors. The submarine is displayed outside, giving the feeling it is ready to go back to sea. The museum, including its submarine, was voted as the 'Favourite monument of the French' by the viewers of a French TV programme in 2022.

This room includes the first jet-powered aircraft made in France, the Leduc ramjet aircraft, and the Griffon, a Mach 3 prototype. Piloted by André Turcat, the prototype featured a hybrid propulsion comprising a ramjet fixed around a reactor. The same architecture was then integrated for the SR-71 Blackbird. Outdoors, the collection encompasses a Rafale demonstrator, an aircraft that was part of the flight display at the Paris Air Show 1986, a Jaguar tactical combat aircraft and Ariane I and Ariane V space launchers. Entrance is free of charge.

Peace Memorial in Caen, Normandy

Some 30 minutes from the landing beaches and Pegasus Bridge, the town of Caen is the home of the *Mémorial de la Paix*. In a high-tech building, visitors can walk throughe chapters of history dedicated to the conflicts of the 20th century, war crimes (notably by National

Socialism) and terrorism and conflicts since 9/11. In a pedagogic approach, special rooms deal with the concentrations camps, war crimes and totalitarian regimes (Japan, Germany and the Soviet Union). The Battle of Normandy is explained in detail in a dynamic attraction. Others booths cover the history of the Manhattan Project, including articles of everyday life affected by the atom bombs of Hiroshima and Nagasaki, this within a comprehensive exhibition on the Second World War. Regarding the Cold War period, a large area in the museum explains the chronology of the Cuban Missile Crisis, with a booth containing pieces of the U-2 spy plane destroyed by a SA-2 missile on 27 October 1961 (a special gift of the Revolution Museum of Havana). In a monumental exhibition room focused on the arms race of the Cold War, visitors can see several pieces of iconic equipment: a MiG 21, the casing of a Mk-28 thermonuclear bomb (a gift of the US Air Force), examples of nuclear protection equipment and a strategic S-3 missile in a mock-up of a launching silo. The city of New York has provided concrete debris of the World Trade Center. These relics echo emotionally with sections of the

Berlin Wall, the fall of which closed a geopolitical cycle. Recently, the Peace Memorial has been enriched with rooms especially devoted to hybrid conflicts which followed the attacks of 9/11 on New York and Washington – in Iraq, Afghanistan, the Middle East and Africa. The Peace Memorial is inspired by a universalist vision, a mirror of the United Nations' principles, allowing visitors to form their own opinion on the central topics of geopolitics. The curators of the museum have included recent examples of militarization around the world, a message that highlights the civilian victims of contemporary wars. The museum has been extended with three memorial gardens: the American Garden, the British Garden and the Canadian Garden, dedicated to the three main allied nations involved in liberating France. A large library is open to the public. The *Mémorial de la Paix* is the most visited museum in France, outside of Paris. The museum, a bit like the Imperial War Museum in London, puts forward a responsible French approach to defence and nuclear deterrence.

10
THE DAY AFTER 8 NOVEMBER 1989

Programmes to modernise and renew France's strategic vectors were already undergoing trials when East Germany opened up the Berlin Wall on 8 November 1989. Would the nuclear strategic concept now be shifted? What was now the purpose of the French nuclear force regarding the hopes of a new world? Would it be necessary to have nuclear bombs in the 'global village', as promoted by images of the fall of the Wall shown on CNN? For many, the atom bomb was the product of the Cold war, and the Cold War was then over. The idea

to reduce the place of nuclear weapons, even to definitely abolish them, then took hold in certain political spheres.

In the early 1990s, the end of the Cold War was acted upon by the Elysée Palace, with defence expenditure having to be reduced, meaning the continuation of research activities became a challenging issue for the military high-tech community. In 1988, Mirage 2000N squadrons were cut by two units, so the FAS could no longer field five, but three squadrons. The number of nuclear attack submarines

A Rafale demonstrator (foreground) with a Mirage 2000: the transition between two generations of combat aircraft, an image of the French air forces for a new century. The Rafale demonstrator was a large-delta winged fighter, with all-moving canards, integrating fly-by-wire flight controls. The aircraft was planned to enter service at the end of the 1990s. (Dassault Aviation)

was also reduced, from 10 vessels to eight and then to just six. The question now was whether the armed forces would have enough money to maintain the line. Considering the new constraints, the three axes were consolidated: the research and development effort on a national scale, under the scrutiny of the DGA, was maintained at only a sufficient level, and the exploitation of civil technologies was encouraged, along with the development of export activities, in view of maintaining the continuity of know-how between the generations. International cooperation was carried out, all the while considering national sovereignty. To reduce costs and develop synergies, industry had to rationalise its assets. The success of the Airbus airliners and Ariane space boosters can be seen as the result of the policy of conversion of military industry decided at a strategic level in the wake of the fall of the Berlin Wall.

Rafale: an air force for the new century

During the 1980s, the Rafale was expected to be the future vector of the airborne deterrence force, from the sea and from air bases. The Rafale was envisaged as accomplishing the missions of six existing combat aircraft: the Mirage III, Mirage F1, Jaguar, Mirage 2000, and carrier-borne Crusader and Super Étendard. Step by step at the Dassault design office, the project was developed during the late 1980s. On 26 January 1988, the joint government committee decided on the official launch of the project. On 27 February 1989, the M88 engine was ignited for the first time. On 23 December 1989, the Ministry of Defence

A model of the *Charles de Gaulle* displayed at the *Salon Naval* of Le Bourget in October 1990. Its air component was composed of Super Étendards and Rafales. (Author's collection).

decided to equip the Navy before the Air Force, its mission being to ensure the air defence of the aircraft carriers. Four prototypes were manufactured to perform testing and development: two marine versions – the single-seaters M01 and M02 – one 'air' version, the C01, and a two-seater B01. The level of specifications was high: in the current environment, the aircraft had to be capable of air-to-air and air-to-ground, reconnaissance, day and night, as well as adverse weather operations. Meanwhile, in 1984, the government had decided to proceed with a combat variant of the ACX Experimental Combat Airplane, due to the conflicting criteria of the respective Future European Fighter nations. Construction of the demonstrator commenced in March 1984, even before a contract was signed with

A Mirage 2000N with its ASMP missile. Initial flight tests of the prototype began on 3 February 1983, and the 2000N entered operational service in 1988 during the last days of the Cold War. Three squadrons formed the core of the French air-based nuclear deterrent until its retirement in 2018, a mission shared with a first nuclear Rafale unit established in 2009. Like the new generation of strategic submarines, the Mirage 2000N embodied the continuation of deterrence through several strategic cycles. (*Armée de l'Air*)

DCNS Brest naval shipyard. It was named *Richelieu* in 1986 by President François Mitterrand, after the famous French statesman Cardinal Richelieu. On 18 May 1987, its name was changed to *Charles de Gaulle* by Jacques Chirac, the Gaullist Prime Minister at the time. By receiving the name of, arguably, one of the greatest Frenchman in history, the programme was engraved in the stone of the French narrative. The *Charles de Gaulle* was to become the Chateau de Versailles of French national defence. It was specified that the ship would have special facilities and equipment to integrate ASMP missiles on board. In 1990, two questions arose: would the programme include a sister ship, as envisaged, and would the production schedule be respected?

Ballistic submarines: the triumph of deterrence

A new generation of nuclear submarines remained a top priority. The new fleet relied on the SNLE-NG, a project entrusted to DCN Cherbourg as, main contractor. The first of the new class was named *Le Triomphant* and was to replace *Le Redoutable*. The contract was signed on 10 March 1986 and work was cleared to begin on 10 July 1987. *Le Triomphant* was followed by two additional units: *Le Temeraire* in 1989 and *Le Vigilant* in 1993. Research work focused on noise reduction, deeper navigation, new sensors and C2 (command and control). Although six vessels had been planned before the fall of the Berlin Wall, the future of the FOST was consolidated, thus guaranteeing for the future the pillars of the deterrence strategy. In a world of uncertainty, France was determined to maintain a credible capability of retaliation.

However, world history was not reduced to the joyous images from Central Europe in the late 1980s with the collapse of communism, just some months of happiness, as on 8 August 1990, Saddam Hussein's Iraq invaded Kuwait shortly after claiming to have a military nuclear programme. The legitimacy of French nuclear deterrence was thus renewed.

the DGA, France's defence procurement agency. The technology demonstrator was rolled out in December 1985 at Saint-Cloud, and took its maiden flight on 4 July 1986 from Istres-le Tubé air base in southern France.

Aircraft carrier: unique and iconic

The ambition of the MoD was to replace both carriers, the *Clemenceau* and *Foch*, with two nuclear-propelled vessels, the option being motivated in part by the oil crisis. In 1977, the design took shape. The hull of the first ship was laid down in April 1989 at the

Le Triomphant, the first in a new generation of strategic submarines and the final achievement of the Cherbourg arsenal, launched in the early 1990s. For its first patrols, *Le Triomphant* was equipped with M-45 MIRV missiles, giving it a circle of deterrence of over 5,000km. The FOST expected the M-5 by the end of the decade, which had twice the range of the older missile system. (Naval Group)

Artist's impression of the M-5 missile project published at the beginning of the 1990s. With a range of 11,000km, this ambitious weapon was designed to be the equivalent of the US Trident IID5. (Aerospatiale/Arianegroup)

This excellent picture of the Licorne nuclear test made on 3 July 1970 offers a strong message of French deterrence and the credibility of its strategy for the future. Nuclear deterrence is a paradox, a message and a manoeuvre, always ready to be used. This image remains to this day confined exclusively to the register of experiments. (CEA)

BIBLIOGRAPHY

Official documents

La dimension radiologique des essais nucléaires français en Polynésie. Ministère de la défense.

La direction des applications militaires. Au cœur de la dissuasion nucléaire française. CEA-EA. Dominique Mongin, William Delahaye (Octobre 2016).

Rafale. Dossier de presse. Dassault Aviation. Direction générale internationale (Juin 2017).

Books

Aron, Raymond, *Le Grand débat. Initiation à la stratégie atomique* (Calmann-Levy, 1963).

Beamont, Hervé, *Avions Nucléaires Français, L'histoire de 1964 à nos Jours* (Éditions ETAI - Sophia, 2016.

Bendjebbar, André *Histoire secrete de la bombe atomique française* (Le Cherche Midi editions, 2000).

Carbonel, J.C., *French Secret Projects: Post-war Fighters* (Crécy Publishing Ltd, 2016).

Cuny, Jean, *Les avions de combat français 1944–1960. Chasse lourde, bombardement, assaut, exploration* (Docavia Larivière, October 1989).

Dassault, Marcel, *Le Talisman* (J'ai lu, 1970).

Delgado, James P., *Nuclear Dawn: The Atomic Bomb from the Manhattan Project to the Cold War* (Osprey Publishing, 2009).

Dumortier, Bernard, *Atolls de l'atome: Mururoa & Fangataufa* (Marines Editions, June 2004).

Dupont, Admiral François, *Commandant de sous-marins. Du Terrible au Triomphant, la vie secrête des sous-marins* (Edition Autrement, 2019).

Géré, François, *La pensée stratégique française contemporaine* (Edition Economica, 2017).

Huwart, Oliver, *Du V2 à Véronique. La naissance des fusées françaises* (Marine Editions, 2004).

Institut Charles-de-Gaulle, Université de Franche-Comté, *L'aventure de la bombe. De Gaulle et la dissuasion nucléaire* (Edition Plon, 1985).

Jane's Fighting ships 1993–94, Ninety-sixth edition, edited by Captain Richard Sharpe RN (Jane's Information Group, 1993).

Jurgensen, Cécile and Mongin, Dominique, *Sous la direction de. Préface de Florence Parly. Ministre des Armées. Résistance et dissuasion. Des origines du programme nucléaire français à nos jours* (Odile Jacob, August 2018).

Laisney, André, *Le Redoutable et l'histoire des technologies des sous-marins* (Marines Editions, 2012).

Loubette, Fabrice, Labrude, Pierre and Antoine, Pierre-Alain, *Les Américains en France. La communication zones et l'OTAN* (Gérard Louis Editeur, 2022).

Notre, Philippe and Vichot, Jean-Louis, *Abécédaire des forces sous-marines* (Edition Decoopman, 2014).

Poirier, Lucien, *Des stratégies nucléaire.* (Hachette, 1977).

Reed, Thomas C., *At the Abyss: An Insider's History of the Cold War* (Ballantine Books, 2005).

Reed, Thomas C. and Stillman, Danny B., *The Nuclear Express: A Political History of the Bomb and its Proliferation* (Ed Zenith Press, 2009).

Schwartz, Stephen I., *Atomic audit: The costs and consequences of US nuclear weapons since 1940* (Brookings Institution Press, 1998).

Soutou, Georges-Henri, *La guerre froide de la France, 1941–1990* (Edition Tallandier, 1918).

Torres, Felix and Däntzer-Kantof, Boris, *Les atomes de la mer. La propulsion nucléaire française – Histoire d'un outil de dissuasion* (Le Cherche Midi Edition, 2022).

Wedin, Lars, *Marianne et Athéna. La pensée militaire française du XVIIIè siècle à nos jours* (Economica, 2011).

Press

'40 ans de dissuasion. Dossier coordonné par l'enseigne de vaisseau Thierry Maguet', *Cols Bleus*, no. 3003 (1 December 2012).

Bovis, Alain, 'La technologie des sous-marins – Sub-marine technology', *Sub-Marines*, July 2016).

Castex, Admiral Raoul, 'Aperçus sur la bombe atomique', *Revue des questions de défense nationale* (October 1945).

Facon, Patrick, 'Dissuasion nucléaire. Les Mirage IV A en alerte', *Le Fana de l'aviation* (October 2014).

Hopkins, Robert, 'Le programme Burning Light. Des essais français sous l'œil des Américains', translated from English by Alexis Rocher, *Le Fana de l'aviation*, no. 573 (August 2017).

Mathe, General Henri, 'Le Mirage IV: père de la guerre électronique en France', *Rubrique Historique de Guerrelec*, no. 5 (June 2005).

Nahmias, Maurice, 'Artillerie nucléaire', *Science et Vie* (January 1946).

Rossigneux, Brigitte, 'Les dossiers du Canard', *La force de frappe tranquille* (September 1984).

Vilain, Jacques, 'Les nouvelles armes tactiques et stratégiques antiforce soviétiques: de futures menaces pour le plateau d'Albion', *Défense & Armement* (February 1987).

Websites

Anfas *(association nationale des Fas)*: www.anfas.fr

Amicale des sous-mariniers: www.agasm.fr

CEA : www.cea.fr

Fondation pour la recherche stratégique : www.frstrategie.org

Ican France: www.icanfrance.fr

Mer & Marine : www.meretmarine.com

Ministère des armées: www.defense.gouv.fr

Special thanks to

Hervé Beaumont; Jean Castanier (Editions Decoopman); Guillaume Belan (press officer at Onera); Mathieu Durand (press officer), Luc Berger and Cyril Cosmao (communication team, Dassault Aviation); Admiral François Dupont; François Géré (president of *Institut Français d'Analyse Stratégique*); Jean-Michel Guhl for the translations of the first chapters; Admiral Jean-François Morel (*rédacteur en chef de la revue Défense*); the communication team of *La Cité de la Mer*; press officers of the *Forces Aériennes Stratégiques*; Alexis Rocher, chief editor of *Le Fana de l'aviation*; Colonel (R) Pierre-Alain Antoine (French Air Force); the press department of Naval Group; Valéry Rousset, military expert.

By the same author:

Dictionnaire de la dissuasion (Marine éditions, September 2011).

Essai nucléaire: la force de frappe Française au XXIè siècle (Lavauzelle), 2014 (prix Vauban, 2015).

Guerre froide épisode II. Dissuasion et diplomatie à l'épreuve (Lavauzelle, 2016).

Hiroshima et Nagasaki, notre héritage nucléaire (Ouest France, 2014)

La dissuasion nucléaire française – dictionnaire d'un recit national (Edition Decoopman, 2019).

ABOUT THE AUTHOR

Philippe Wodka-Gallien

A 1990 graduate of the Institut d'Etudes Politiques de Paris, or Sciences Po Paris, Philippe Wodka-Gallien is a member of the Institut Français d'Analyse Stratégique, a think-tank in Paris. A French citizen, he is an auditor of the 47th National Session of the IHEDN (Institut des Hautes Etudes de Défense Nationale), in the Chapter concerned with armament and the defence economy. In 2015, he produced a collective work concerning military nuclear power (a strategic perspective), edited by Revue Défense Nationale. The same year, he received the IHEDN Vauban Prize for his book *Essai nucléaire. La force de frappe française au XXIe siècle : défis, ambitions et stratégie.*

His expertise stems from a career of more than 30 years in the aeronautics, space and defence industry. A regular contributor to *Revue Défense Nationale*, a historian of military issues, he is the author of numerous articles in the following magazines: *Air Zone, Le Fana de l'Aviation, Journal of Electronic Defense,* and in *Revue Défense Nationale*, the Union-IHEDN magazine.